TOLERATION

PORTRAIT OF JOHN BIGELOW BY FEDOR ENCKE
PAINTED IN 1900
THIS PORTRAIT HANGS IN THE GREAT HALL OF THE CHAMBER OF
COMMERCE OF THE STATE OF NEW YORK, HAVING BEEN PRESENTED TO
THE CHAMBER BY MAJOR JOHN BIGELOW AND MISS GRACE BIGELOW.
Reproduced by Permission.

TOLERATION
and other essays and studies

POSTHUMOUS

BY
JOHN BIGELOW

WITH AN INTRODUCTION
BY GLENN FRANK

With what judgment shall we judge one another?

Essay Index Reprint Series

 BOOKS FOR LIBRARIES PRESS
FREEPORT, NEW YORK

First Published 1927
Reprinted 1969

STANDARD BOOK NUMBER:
8369-1075-3

LIBRARY OF CONGRESS CATALOG CARD NUMBER:
78-84298

PRINTED IN THE UNITED STATES OF AMERICA

Progress depends very largely on the encouragement of variety. Whatever tends to standardize the community, to establish fixed and rigid modes of thought, tends to fossilize society. * * * It is the ferment of ideas, the clash of disagreeing judgments, the privilege of the individual to develop his own thoughts and shape his own character, that makes progress possible. It is not possible to learn much from those who uniformly agree with us. But many useful things are learned from those who disagree with us; and even when we can gain nothing our differences are likely to do us no harm.

CALVIN COOLIDGE.

CONTENTS

INTRODUCTION

INTRODUCTION

I HAVE embraced with an eager willingness the invitation to write a foreword to this study of toleration found among Mr. Bigelow's papers, despite the fact that I do not agree with all its contentions and implications.

I am not greatly interested in the theological matrix in which Mr. Bigelow fixed his forceful plea for toleration. I do not believe with him that the variations of Protestantism are its strength or that they have sprung from the womb of a wide tolerance. I believe that the variations of Protestantism are its weakness and that they have been born of intolerance. And at the moment I doubt that the orthodox Protestantism of America can boast any greater authentic tolerance than the Catholicism of America.

And yet, despite these reservations, I cannot allow to slip through my fingers an opportunity to add whatever force I can to a volume that pleads for tolerance in this intolerant time.

Bigotry is the mark of a barbarous people; tolerance is the touchstone of civilization. We Americans, of all men, cannot fight for even one hour in the ranks of intolerance without turning traitor to the founders of the republic who gave their lives to the task of invoking the ideals and fashioning the forms of government that would give the human spirit a chance to stretch its wings unhampered alike by ruthless kings and thoughtless mobs. And, as individuals, we can never achieve inner peace and power until we have become at least acolytes at the altar of tolerance.

What we do to our critics is, in the end, more a judgment upon ourselves than a judgment upon them. The greatness of American civilization will finally be determined by our ability to be grateful for irritating criticism, for a nation cannot kill its critics without killing its character. For a while the ancient Greek civilization was a great and glowing civilization; but one day it suddenly shrivelled into littleness and killed its major critic—Socrates. And by that blunder ancient Greece proved that a civilization cannot have a thin skin and a great soul at the same time. Nothing is more important than our learning how to be sensitive to criticism without becoming intolerant of critics.

"If you put me to death," said Socrates to the Athenians who were clamoring for his execution, "you will not easily find another man to fill my place. God has sent me to attack the city, as if it were a great and noble horse which was rather sluggish from its size, and which needed to be aroused by a gadfly; and I think that I am the gadfly that God has sent to the city to attack it; for I never cease from settling upon you, and rousing, and exhorting, and reproaching each man of you all day long. You are vexed, as drowsy persons are, when they are awakened, and of course you could easily kill me with a single blow, and then sleep on undisturbed for the rest of your lives, unless God were to care for you enough to send another man to arouse you."

The Athenians did not take his advice. Socrates was sentenced to die by drinking a cup of hemlock. The Athenians thought they were simply getting rid of a disturber of their peace; what they were really doing was drowning a whole civilization in one small cup of hemlock. This is not a mere rehearsal of ancient history. There are State Legislatures just now which, in their attempt to convert their State Universities into retail stores dispensing majority opinions only, are repeating this Athenian method of social suicide. But such episodes are and must be kept exceptions. America must not blunder as Athens blundered.

There is an increasing tendency upon the part of Americans to choose between the flaming fanaticisms of bigotry and the sentimental surrenders of indifference, while the time cries aloud for men in whom earnest personal conviction and generous tolerance meet and merge.

Introduction

America needs a new birth of the spirit manifested by Voltaire when, in a letter to Helvetius, he said, "I wholly disapprove of what you say, and will defend to the death your right to say it." We must learn to respect even a man's right to think wrong.

I hope that this tardy publication of Mr. Bigelow's essay will help a little toward such a new birth of tolerance.

GLENN FRANK.

Madison, Wisconsin.

TOLERATION

CHAPTER I

THE world makes too little account of the startling fact that no two persons are or ever were entirely of the same opinion upon any subject. The desire to have others adopt our opinions, and our impatience at their refusal are nearly as universal. Hence, sects, parties, controversies, litigation, alienation of kindred and friends, penal legislation, brawls, wars, and in fact pretty much every disturbance of the harmony of human society. How few people can discuss any question from opposite sides with a single eye to reaching the truth, with entire exemption from pride of opinion and the promptings of personal interest! How large the proportion who are only restrained by the fear of the police from attempting to compel uniformity by violence! This is especially the case with that large class in all countries whose command of logic and language is not sufficient adequately to express the strength of their convictions or the temperature of their feelings. The learned man gets out of patience with the arguments of the ignorant, the logical

I

with the arguments of the scatter-brain, the school teacher with his blundering pupils, the parent with the indocility of his children. And in every case there is an impulse on each side to impose its views on the other, usually limited only by considerations in which any recognition of the right and propriety of everyone's adhering to his own opinions while they are his own is conspicuous by its absence.

It would be a grievous mistake, however, to suppose that this propensity to constrain others to share our opinions, to go to our church, to vote with our party and "run with our machine" is an evil, and for evil only good. So far from such being the case, it is—humanly speaking—the mainspring of all human progress. The desire to have our own opinions prevail is the chief incentive with us to study to form right opinions and to buttress them with sound, or at least plausible reasons. Every educational institution, every printing press, every sect and party in the world owes its existence to this innate and universal ambition to make other people think and act as we do, or would like to do. But, like all the virtues, it may be, is now, and has always been by everyone at times expanded into a vice, when its results are as revolting and disastrous as when, exercised under wise limitations, its results are beneficent.

In insisting upon others' conforming their opinions to ours, we overlook the vital fact that no one's opinions would answer the purpose of anyone but himself. We may by example and precept help a man to change his opinions, but until he does change them for ours, our opinions would not benefit him, and it would be impossible to impose them upon him.

It is natural for us to think our opinions correct and opinions in conflict with them erroneous. It is as natural that we should desire those we love, or in whose opinions we have any interest, to forsake their opinions and adopt ours as it would be calamitous for us were it otherwise. The error—and it is an error from which no one, probably, is entirely exempt—consists in assuming that it would be better if all the world were altogether of our opinion, or that diversity of opinions is any more to be regretted than diversity in the products of the earth, in the color of flowers, or in the reproductive habits of animals. To this delusion, perhaps, more of the misery, crime, and disasters of our race may be traced than to any other. Its worst results have been chiefly conspicuous in the sphere of religious opinions. Nor is this strange, as our opinions on religious subjects, more than on any other, are presumed to influence our fortunes, not only in time but through eternity. Hence it is that in the name of religion the world has always proved most intolerant.

Toleration is commonly regarded as the converse of intolerance, and the tolerant person, party or government as the very opposite of the intolerant. In point of fact, however, the difference between toleration, intolerance and persecution is simply one of degree. In whatever we tolerate we assume the right not to tolerate. We tolerate a man, a party, or a sect with which we are not in accord, but we never speak of tolerating opinions in harmony with our own, or opinions in harmony with those of the party or sect to which we are espoused. Intolerance assumes the right to refuse what toleration assumes the right to grant. President Madison was instrumental in having the words, "fullest toleration" stricken out of the original Bill of Rights of his native state, as smacking of intolerance.[1] It is a curious and

---

[1] The bill as originally reported ran as follows: "That religion or the duty we owe to our Creator, and the manner of discharging it, can be directed only by reason and conviction, not by force or violence; and therefore that all men should enjoy the fullest toleration in the exercise of religion, according to the dictates of conscience, unpunished and unrestrained by the magistrates unless," etc.

Madison's amendment ran as follows: "That religion, or the duty we owe our Creator and the manner of discharging it, being under the direction of reason and religion only, not of violence or compulsion, according to the dictates of conscience, and, therefore, that no man or class of men ought, on account of religion, to be invested with peculiar emoluments or privileges, nor subjected to any penalties or disabilities unless," etc.

4

pregnant illustration of the superior importance, in the world's esteem, of our opinions
upon religious subjects to those which we entertain upon other subjects that, while there is a
great deal of intolerance in human society
about matters of more or less general concern,
religion and its coefficients are practically the
only subjects strictly within the domain of
private opinion, the toleration of which nations
have undertaken to limit or guarantee by law.

Quite as large a proportion of human society
as that of which its religious sects are composed
have succumbed to the despotism of fashion,
have felt constrained to wear the reigning
dynastic or partisan colors of the period, or to
drift with its prevailing scientific and humanitarian movements, but it is only in an incidental
and indirect way that government or society
has ever attempted to interfere with the free
exercise of opinion on these subjects. There is,
however, the germ of intolerance in everything

As this amendment amounted to instant and complete disestablishment, it proved too radical for the
convention, but the principle of it was finally adopted
in the following terms: "That religion, or the duty
we owe to our Creator, and the manner of discharging
it, can be directed only by reason and conviction, not
by force or violence, and therefore all men are equally
entitled to the free exercise of religion, according to
the dictates of conscience, and that it is the duty of
all to practise Christian forbearance, love and charity
towards each other."

we tolerate in another. We may treat the teachers and disciples of every religious sect with equal respect and consideration and yet be very intolerant towards those who occupy a lower or a higher rank in our social sphere, who pay too little or too much respect to prevailing fashions, whose modes of life are more worldly or less worldly than ours. But Toleration and Intolerance are words rarely used except in reference to religious opinions and the modes of their display.

It is now some two centuries since the famous Bishop of Meaux dealt what his coreligionists are wont to consider a fatal blow at Protestantism by the publication of his *Variations of the Protestant Church.* Taking for his point of departure the principle that there is but one Lord, one Faith and one Baptism; that the Holy Spirit sheds only pure light and that the truth it teaches holds a uniform language, he maintained that there was no uniformity of creed or dogma among the manifold sects of Protestantism and therefore that the Protestant church not only could not be the true church but that all Protestants were necessarily Gentiles or Heretics. He maintained that, on the other hand, the Latin church, of which he was an eminent dignitary, had remained complete and perfect as it came from the hands of the Lord and His disciples; that it had undergone no change, and had been from

6

the beginning unintermittingly guarded from error by the Holy Spirit.

In this doctrine that the Latin church is the only gate of heaven, its hierarchy have found not only a pretext but what they profess to regard as the equivalent of a command to prescribe and persecute heresy and to offer every species of carnal or worldly as well as spiritual inducements to those they call heretics to purge themselves of their heresy and to unite with the only church which can insure salvation. Persecution and bribery have always been as well recognized agencies for rescuing heretics from the perils of heresy and bringing them under the shelter of the Latin church as the ministrations of the pulpit or the exposition of the sacred writings. "The Prince," says Bossuet, "is the protector of the public peace, which rests on religion, and ought to sustain his throne, of which religion is the foundation. Those who do not wish the Prince permitted to use rigor in religious matters, because religion ought to be free, are in an impious error. Otherwise it would be necessary to tolerate among all subjects and states, idolatry, Mahomedanism, Judaism, every false religion, blasphemy, atheism even, and the greatest crimes would enjoy the completest impunity."

It was with the concurrence, if not through the advice of Bossuet, that his sovereign created a national fund for the sole and express pur-

7

pose of seducing to desert their Protestant communion, and employed a no inconsiderable portion of his army in intimidating and harassing into the Latin communion, those whose infidelity to their convictions could not be purchased. It was by these and kindred means and in pursuance of a public policy sanctioned in principle and practice by the highest authority of the period in church and state, that the neighboring states of Switzerland, Germany, Holland and Great Britain became cities of refuge for the persecuted Protestants of France and the seats of new industries by which they were enriched and by which France lost more than half a million of her most ingenious and virtuous citizens.

Even the gentle Fenelon could not see his way clear, much as he desired it, to leave his countrymen free to take their chance of salvation outside of what he regarded as the only true church. "If it be true," he said, speaking of his old friend Madame Guyon, then shut up in the Bastille for the heresy of Quietism, "If it be true that this woman has sought to establish this damnable system (of Quietism) she should be burned instead of being admitted to the Communion as she has been by M. Meaux."

On another occasion, referring to the means which the Pope ought to suggest to the King for the extirpation of Jansenism, he proposed:

To withhold all pardons or favors from

8

them; to deprive of all employment and dignities whoever should be only suspected of secretly protecting the partisans of Jansenism. To require them in all cases to sign a renunciation of their doctrine. To remove all holders of benefices and all Supervisors of religious Communities who should refuse to sign such renunciation. To excommunicate all the contumacious after three Catholic admonitions. To treat as relapsed heretics all who, after having signed, should attempt to evade their engagement by any reserves whatever.

There was but one if any penalty known to the criminal law of France in those days more severe than awaited a relapsed convert from Protestantism.

It was considered quite a hopeful indication of enlarging charity that the oath taken recently by an English Roman Catholic in assuming the Pallium was purged of the words: *"Haereticos, schismaticos et rebelles eidem Domino nostro, vel successoribus praedictis, pro posse persequar et impugnabo."* [1]

It would be a yet more hopeful sign of Christian charity if this clause were omitted from the oaths of archbishops in countries where the Roman Catholic is the predominant Christian faith as well as in countries where archbishops

---

[1] "I will so far as possible pursue and war upon heretics, schismatics and rebels against the same our Master [*i.e.*, the Pope] and his aforesaid successors.'

would in no case be permitted to pursue and worry heretics and schismatics in the name of religion.

Nor has this intolerance been confined to any particular Christian sect. Yielding to an impulse which seems to prompt everyone to magnify his office, the priesthood of all or most religious denominations calling themselves Christians, have insisted with more or less pertinacity upon the dogma that redemption through Christ was not the privilege of all, but was confined to those who had and have "the outward knowledge thereof" in order to the obtaining of its saving effect; and therefore that damnation was the inevitable destination of all who had dwelt outside of the church. The Remonstrants of Holland professed these views and Protestantism as well as Romanism has not hesitated, according to the measure of its strength, to recruit its ranks by the persecution of dissent. It may be doubted, even at this day, whether there is not as much energy expended by the clergy in an effort to prove that all outside of the Christian church will be damned, as in showing how those within its fold may be saved.

John Locke, one of the most advanced champions of religious freedom that Europe has produced up to this time, spent some years in France shortly after the Revocation of the Edict of Nantes and was familiar with the terrors and oppressions which ensued, but he was unable entirely to surrender the government's right to persecute for opinion's sake. He held that the State cannot tolerate any sect that teaches that men are not obliged to keep their engagements, or that princes may be dethroned by those differing with them upon religious problems. Neither would he tolerate any sect which professed to owe service to or claimed the protection of any other prince than the one under whom they lived, or who denied the existence of a God.

These exceptions were aimed chiefly if not exclusively at Catholics and atheists, who yet constitute no inconsiderable proportion of the population of the civilized world.

The difference between the Tolerance—the charity, rather—of Locke and that of Bossuet is one rather of degree than of kind, and when applied to actual affairs would be found *mutatis mutandis* to lead to about the same results.

While admitting the contemporaneous intolerance of Protestant countries, it is important here to signalize one conspicuous exception. As early as 1675 David Barclay presented to Charles II. his "Apology for the true Christian Religion as Preached by the people called Quakers," in which, for the first time I believe in the literature of Europe, the doctrine of freedom of conscience is proclaimed in all its length and breadth and height and depth and without

reservation and qualification, and sustained by
such a grasp of thought and force of argument
that no casuist in the interests of Church or
State has ever been able to disturb it.[1]

---

[1] There is a touching eloquence in the following passage with which Barclay concludes his XIVth proposition "Concerning the Power of the Civil Magistrate
in Matters purely Religious and Pertaining to the
Conscience." Few words have come down to us from
that age more abounding in the eloquence of wisdom
and earnestness. It is difficult to read these words
even now, after the lapse of two centuries, without
emotion:

"To conclude this matter, glory to God, and our
Lord Jesus Christ, that, now these twenty-five years,
since we were known to be a distinct and separate
people, He hath given us faithfully to suffer for his
name, without shrinking or fleeing the cross; and what
liberty we now enjoy, it is by His mercy, and not by
any outward working or procuring of our own, but
it is He has wrought upon the hearts of our opposers.
Nor was it any outward interest hath procured it unto
us, but the testimony of our harmlessness in the hearts
of our superiors: for God hath preserved us hitherto
in the patient suffering of Jesus, that we have not
given away our cause by persecuting any, which few
if any Christians that I know, can say. Now against
our unparalleled yet innocent and Christian cause,
our malicious enemies have nothing to say, but that,
if we had power, we should do likewise. This is a
piece of mere unreasonable malice, and a privilege
they take to judge of things to come, which they have
not by immediate revelation; and surely it is the
greatest height of harsh judgment to say men would
do contrary to their professed principle if they could,
who have from their practice hitherto given no ground
for it, and wherein they only judge others by themselves: such conjectures cannot militate against us,
so long as we are innocent. And if ever we prove

12

"Since God hath assumed to himself," says Barclay, "the power and dominion of the Conscience, who alone can rightly instruct and govern it, therefore it is not lawful for any whatsoever, by virtue of any authority or principality they bear in the government of this world, to force the consciences of others; and therefore all killing, banishing, fining, imprisoning, and other such things which are inflicted upon men for the alone exercise of their conscience, or difference in worship or opinion, proceedeth from the spirit of Cain the murderer, and is contrary to the truth; providing always, that no man, under the pretence of conscience, prejudice his neighbour in his life or estate, or do any thing destructive to, or inconsistent with human society; in which case the law is for the transgressor, and justice is to be administered upon all, without respect of persons."

Baxter in his Holy Commonwealth pronounced universal toleration "Soul murder," and he knew something, by experience, of sectarian intolerance.

Milton, the apostle of toleration in his day, excepts the Roman Catholics on the ground that their worship is idolatrous and the Old Testament forbids the toleration of idolatry.

---

guilty of persecution, by forcing other men by corporal punishment to our way, then let us be judged the greatest of hypocrites, and let not any spare to persecute us. Amen, saith my soul."

Could Milton have been so blind as not to see that on his principle, the idolaters who always constituted a majority of our race, would have been warranted in persecuting the Christian minority back into idolatry or into the holy army of martyrs?

CHAPTER II

WHILE Louis XIV was looking after the spiritual interests of his subjects in the way we have described, Maria Theresa was similarly employed in a neighboring State. The sweetness of this princess's nature has been much extolled by historians, because she shed tears when she felt constrained to add to her Dominions a part of Poland, though her tears did not prevent her retaining it. In 1769 she also undertook a reform of her criminal code. She so far gave way to her feminine sympathies as to retain but six forms of torture. These were: crushing the fingers; crushing the toes; exposure on a ladder; burning the bosom with six candles; the Spanish boot which crushed the legs; suspension by the arms while supporting enormous weights attached to the feet. Among the crimes which these instrumentalities were designed to punish were, the seduction of a Christian from his faith by a Jew, blasphemy, and magic, provided commerce with the devil was proven.

This seems very horrible to us as we read it by the light of modern civilization, or even by the darkness of modern rationalism, and people sometimes forget themselves so far as to doubt whether the Inquisition of Dominic was operated by beings of our own species. It was, however, and still is, operated by precisely the same species. Nor is it easy to see how Protestants or any other churchmen can justify themselves for not relying more even than they usually have done upon the efficacy of persecution and bribery, if they believe as they must— to justify an appeal to selfish and carnal inducements of any kind—that their particular church is the exclusive repository of saving truth, and that eternal misery awaits all who die outside of its embrace, or if they adhere, as most of what are known as orthodox churches do, to the theory that the Sacraments confer grace, *ex opere operato,* and that this act of submission to the laws of one's church and not any real inward change, is what justifies him.

As this doctrine of unity and uniformity of belief in the church as a condition of salvation, so elaborately urged by Bossuet, has been systematically taught and insisted upon as an article of faith by the Latin church; as it prevails to a greater or less degree in most of the religious organizations of our epoch; as it has been the source of incalculable anxiety and distress, and as it is to-day one of the most serious obstacles to the restoration of saving health to all nations, it may be well to point out the fallacy, if there be one, upon which it has thrived

16

so long and continues to thrive. In doing this let us see also if we cannot find a rational excuse and justification for the infinite diversity of opinions in matters of faith which always has and doubtless always will prevail in this World of Time.

The by no means antiquated notions that the sun revolved around the earth, that our planet rested on the back of a tortoise, that comets and eclipses were special heralds of Divine wrath to men, that magical powders and holy water were efficacious for driving away the foul fiend, were not greater delusions than the doctrine which the illustrious Bishop of Meaux made the postulate of his famous essay. He could have taken no position more fatal to his argument for the altogether human and corrupt origin of Protestantism than by making uniformity and immutability in matters of faith a test of the true Church on earth.

It may not have been very generally known in the days of Bossuet, but it will scarcely be contested seriously now, that no two things ever will come from the hand of their Creator precisely alike. The Master never duplicates anything. Neither could any two things ever become precisely alike, without ceasing to be two. It is equally certain that no human being was ever, for two consecutive moments, in precisely the same relations to all if to any other objects. The law of change in every human being is as inexorable and as perpetual in its operation as that which leads the planets in their eternal dance. The saintly George Herbert seems to have had this changeableness of man in his mind when he wrote:

"Oh, what a thing is man! how farre from power,
    From settled peace and rest!
He is some twentie severall men at least
    Each severall hour."

. Our notions of right and wrong, that is our sense of duty, must vary in some degree with every variation in the sum of our knowledge and experience. Every act or incident in our lives is our answer, consciously or unconsciously, to the one vital and the only vital question, which is perpetually addressed to us by the external conditions of our lives: "Will you do what you think is right, or what you think is wrong?" Our answer, whatever it may be, invariably lands us upon a higher or lower spiritual plane, but never on precisely the same as that which we occupied before it was made. The power of resisting the temptations which are perpetually welling up from our lower, unregenerated nature has been either increased or diminished. As no one stands in precisely the same relations to his environment for two consecutive moments, his answers must be liable to variations corresponding with the inevitable and perpetual variations of his spiritual state. The amount of truth that

18

he will appropriate to himself from each of these moral respirations, will always depend upon the amount of error he deliberately and from a genuine love of truth may displace; for obviously, nothing can be accepted by anyone as truth that does not displace or exterminate the corresponding error. We cannot appropriate the Copernican truth without the extermination of the Ptolemaic and every other theory which cannot be reconciled with the revolution of the earth around the sun. Every incident in our lives is presumptively such an addition to our stock of truths and such a diminution of our stock of ignorance and error that we cannot be supposed to remain for any appreciable period of time upon the same spiritual plane, or to hold precisely the same views of our duty. A gifted English writer who has recently found his way into the Latin communion says:[1]

"The only objection then that can be urged from without against intolerance, is that on religious matters there is no certainty attainable; and intolerance is only decried in the present day because it is a protest against this opinion. . . . The great point to remember is, that intolerance is but one facet of all certain beliefs that have any practical import; and thus it can only be condemned on one or both of the two following grounds: That religious beliefs are

---

[1] *The Nineteenth Century,* Jan., 1879, "The Logic of Toleration," by W. H. Mallock.

either essentially uncertain, or that they are essentially unimportant." This doctrine seems to assume what persecution always must assume, that one view or belief only, *quo ad* the believer, can be right, and that every other belief inconsistent with that must be in conflict with the truth as it is in him. This is a mistake, as applied to human judgment. No two men have ever seen truth in precisely the same proportions; nor does one of us see truth in precisely the same proportions for any considerable length of time. Among finite beings all truth is relative. Absolute truth is not attainable by the human intellect; nor could any human intellect comprehend it.

Among the theses sustained at Dijon in France in the latter part of the 17th century, the Jesuits laid down the following proposition:[1]

"That philosophic sin is a human act contrary to nature and to reason, but that this sin, however grievous, if committed by one who has no knowledge of God or who did not actually think of Him, is not an offense against God which merits eternal punishment."

---

[1] Que le péché philosophique est une action humaine contraire à la nature et à la raison: Mais que ce péché quelque grief qu'il puisse être, étant commis par celui qui n'a point de connaissance de Dieu ou qui n'y pense point actuellement, n'est point une offense de Dieu, ni qui mérite la peine eternelle.

This thesis was censured at Louvain in 1688. The Jesuits responded in the farther proposition:[1]

"Although the existence of God may be demonstrated, it may happen that a person aided only by the ordinary gifts of grace may be ignorant of it, without being in fault. Let the persecutors of the doctrine of philosophic sin taught at Dijon, ruin this proposition if they can."

Upon this, Basnage, the champion Protestant of his day, remarks:

"By this doctrine it appears that the Jesuits accept as a principle that an act is not free and voluntary so as to involve guilt in its author, unless he knows the sin of it and actually thinks of it. Hence it follows that if God does not soften the hardness of heart that is contracted by inveterate habit, and if one let himself give way to his passions without reflection, he does not sin according to the Jesuits. So soon as a man shall have stifled his reason which enables him to discern good and evil, he may commit all sorts of crimes with impunity. One of the poets has said that as long as a wicked person is traversed by such reflections,

---

[1] Quoique l'existence de Dieu puisse etre démontrée, il se peut faire qu'elle soit ignorée par un homme aidé seulement des secours ordinaires de la grace, sans qu'il y ait de sa faute: que les persécuteurs de la doctrine du péché philosophique enseignée a Dijon ruinent, s'ils peuvent, cette proposition.

" 'Il a vers l'innocence encore quelque penchant,
C'est toujours dans le coeur où le crime domine,
De la virtu bannie un reste de racine.
Mais on est sans retour quand on est sans combats;
L'absence des remors est dans un coeur coupable
D'un tyran achevé, la marque indubitable.'

"But," adds Basnage, "according to the morals of the Jesuits a profound hardening of the heart is the state most sure. As soon as one has got so much the better of his faith as to think no more of God, all goes well. No more half sinners who have yet some remnants of goodness and who resist their passions. The finished sinners who live in a continual pursuit of pleasure, whose career is never interrupted by the least remorse, may brave hell; all their crimes are philosophic sins which do not offend God nor merit external punishment.[1]

Though Jesuit casuistry has unhappily never been above suspicion, the society certainly had its Protestant adversary in this instance at a disadvantage. Basnage is obliged to pervert the Jesuits' meaning to maintain his position. "So soon," he says, "as a man shall have stifled his reason which enables him to discern good and evil, he may commit all sorts of crimes with impunity." But the very act of stifling his reason so as to disqualify him from discerning good from evil, was as an overt evil

---

[1] Histoire des Ouvrages des Savants, 1689, p. 543.

22

act; it was therefore within the category of acts which, according to the Jesuits, constituted an offense meriting eternal punishment. The act of stifling the reason implies resistance, implies the power of discriminating between right and wrong, and a determination to do wrong in spite of the knowledge that it is wrong. That is precisely not the case supposed and excused by the Jesuits.

In point of fact—and of this none of us should ever lose sight though all of us do, no one being in possession of absolute truth about anything — there is nothing in the heavens above nor in the earth beneath nor in the waters under the earth, about which we are not liable to learn something tomorrow to modify our opinions of today; and the day after, to learn something to modify our opinions of tomorrow. From the cradle to the grave, with every increment of knowledge our opinions change. Our opinions last adopted we always think are correct, and yet they may prove to be little if any nearer absolute truth than those entertained in our infancy.

The chemistry and science of yesterday may be as obsolete tomorrow as the thaumaturgy of the Middle Ages; our tools, our instruments, the greatest triumphs of our art, skill and taste, are already on their way to the museums of the virtuosi. The student of astronomy must begin by learning that there is no east or

west, no up or down, no centre or circumfer-
ence; that there is no absolute point in space.
The microscope and the telescope force us to
the conclusion that there is no such thing as
size in the absolute sense of the word. In fact,
the human mind is not capable of formulating
any absolute truth. It may stretch forth in
many directions and between two statements
sometimes determine which is nearer the truth
or relatively the truer. Beyond that it is not
given finite minds to go.

Dieu n'a scellé dans l'homme aucune certitude,
Tout corps traine son ombre et tout esprit sa doute.

"Who lights the fagot?" asks Cardinal Pole,
in Tennyson's play of "Queen Mary," and he
answers his own question by saying, "Not the
firm faith but the lurking doubt."

No two persons worship precisely the same
God, nor does anyone constantly worship the
same God. Every man's God is his Ideal, and
that changes more or less every day.

In a sense the modern Christian is as much
a pantheist and worships as many gods in the
course of his life as the contemporary of Plato
or of Marcus Aurelius did. Were every
clergyman of the Christian church, not to speak
of laymen, to describe in minute detail all the
attributes of the God he worships, not using

the technical knowledge of theology but giving the exact image of the God that is impressed on his heart and as that interior image is manifested in his life from day to day—we should have a Pantheon to which that described by Hesiod in his Theogony would bear no comparison in respect either to number or variety, nor would their divinities have as much the advantage of the gods of Pagan Greece and Rome in the attributes with which they would prove to be invested, as we are disposed to flatter ourselves.

Of the infinitely various conceptions of the Divine personality it is each individual's part and duty to decide, not which is the true one —for the true one in His fullness is incomprehensible to everyone—but the one which seems most nearly true *to him*. He is responsible for the direction in which he travels, not for what he shall see or experience on his journey. The Lord's resurrection symbolizes our own rising from gross material conceptions of the purposes of life to higher planes of existence. Our places in that world which we are all soon to enter, will be determined by the ideas we form here of the King of Kings, that is by our Ideals; by the resurrection or degradation of our conception of the Perfect One. But that Ideal, those conceptions, are as constantly changing as our physical bodies.

Toleration

Nor should we ever lose sight of the fact that our environment is adjusted, not by us, but by Providence; not according to our wishes or judgment, but according to our spiritual state or condition at the moment. That environment must be the best for all of us until we change ourselves; we may use every effort to change our neighbor from what we regard as the error of his ways, but we may not interfere with his freedom. As no two stomachs crave precisely the same diet nor possess precisely the same powers of digestion, neither do any two souls require precisely the same spiritual aliment; nor do any of us know precisely the kind we most require. The Master does, and He regulates our environment with unerring wisdom to secure for us the best of which we have made ourselves capable.

"You look to the sky at evening, and out of the depths
 of blue
A little star, you call it, is glimmering faintly through.
Little? He sees, who looks from His throne in the
 highest place,
A great world, circling grandly the limitless realms
 of space.

So with your life's deep purpose, set in His mighty
 plan,
Out of the dark you see it, looking with human scan.
Little and weak you call it. He from his throne may
 see
Issues that move on grandly into eternity.

Toleration

Sow the good seed, and already the harvest may be
 won.
The deed is great in the doing, that God calls good
 when done.
'Tis as great perhaps to be noble as noble things to do;
And the world of men is better, if one man grows
 more true.

Let us be strong in the doing, for that is ours alone;
The meaning and end are His, and He will care for
 his own.
And, if it seems to us little, remember that from afar
He looks into a world where we but glance at a star."

CHAPTER III

IF we can never attain absolute truth; if we are only relatively right according to our lights, which of course vary with our age and environment, we can, of course, only be made accountable for the quota of light accorded to us and the use we make of it, for no one knows the absolute truth, therefore no one can do what is absolutely right. There is no one so degraded as to have no notion of a Supreme Being, the Institutor of the system of laws for the government of the world which yields more happiness and more satisfactory results to those who obey them than to those who violate them; nor is anyone so wise or so pure or so good as always to obey those laws, or to live up to or anywhere near to their provisions. Everyone therefore must be judged by the lights that he has, and the use that he makes of them. To judge him by any other standard would be as absurd as to apply the provisions of our criminal law to an infant, to a maniac or to an idiot.

If this light, this knowledge of what is true and good, originated with us; if we could of ourselves generate as much or as little of it as

28

we pleased, then of course we should be accountable for every one of our acts that was not in harmony with eternal truth and right. But we cannot originate a ray of the light by which we discern the differences between the right and the wrong. We merely receive and transmit this light, and our minds become luminous only by the rays thus transmitted, as in the material world objects are made visible, not by any light in themselves, but by the light which they transmit or reflect. The light of our sun is pure white, but when it falls upon natural objects it is reflected in various colors according to the state or quality of the reflecting surface.

There is a fraternity of weakness, crime and wretchedness to which everyone who has ever in any degree been weak, who has ever done wrong, who has ever been unhappy, belongs. It is in recognition of this brotherhood that we are not to cast stones against those who are condemned for their evil deeds. The criminal is our brother, not only because the Divine image has been impressed upon him as well as upon us, but because that image has been perverted by us as well as by him. The degree of iniquity, differing as it does in each, makes no difference with the truth of this general law. If we are capable of sinning at all, it is only a question of the degree of temptation that will determine the greatness of the

crime we are liable to commit. We are not to
forget that we are ourselves sinners whenever
we contemplate wrongs in others. The slight-
est weakness in us reveals to us our relationship
with all that is iniquitous, and calls upon us to
recognize as brothers and as sisters all who
are weak and sinful; and it is hence that the
Lord says to us, "Let him that is without sin"—
that is, no one of us—"first cast a stone at
her," that is, sit in judgment upon the sinner.

Even "Solomon loved the Lord, walking in
the statutes of David his father; only he sacri-
ficed and burned incense in the high places."
Also, while building the house of the Lord and
the wall of Jerusalem, "He made affinity with
Pharaoh, king of Egypt, and took Pharaoh's
daughter and brought her into the City of
David" until he made an end of his building.

"Enter not into judgment with thy servant,
O Lord," said the Psalmist, "for in thy sight
shall no man living be justified." (*Psalm cxliii.*
2.)

It was Jesus also who said, "There is none
good but one, that is God."

As applied to ourselves this means that none
of us possesses any goodness that he can call
his own. The loveliest traits of character that
we seem to have, so far as we possess them
from self and use them for the sake of self, are
not good. No matter how heavenly we may
appear in our disposition, no matter how we

30

have been blessed in the natural and spiritual affairs of our lives, no matter how we may be loved and praised among men, there is no real goodness in us that is self-derived. "There is none good." And this applies not only to the goodness we already seem to own, but to that which may yet be vouchsafed us. We cannot attain any goodness from self. We not only are not good; we cannot become good in this way.

That "there is none good," means therefore in a word in reference to ourselves, that we neither have nor can have from self any goodness whatever. "There is none good but one, that is God." He is the Source from which all goodness is derived. He is the "true Light, which lighteth every man that cometh into the world," of which the John the Baptist was sent to bear witness. When that Light falls upon the human mind, it is of course absolute truth, but it is received and refracted according to the spiritual condition of the recipient, in no two individuals taking precisely the same hue. This modification of Divine truth in passing through our minds is what we may claim as our own work. The truth is all the Lord's; its modification only is our property, just as the color which any object in nature reflects is described as its peculiar color. To judge Plato or Socrates, who had probably never heard of Jehovah, and certainly had not heard of Christ, by the standards we would apply to a philosopher of the Nineteenth Century, would be like censuring a white rose for not being red, or a lion for not grazing like a sheep.

The ever changing standard of truth among men has found an admirable and impressive illustration in the errors into which a man on board ship is liable to fall in trying to state the direction in which he supposes he is traveling.[1]

"Here, for instance, is a ship which for simplicity's sake we may suppose to be anchored at the equator, and headed to the west. When the captain walks from stem to stern, in what direction does he move? East, is the obvious answer, an answer which for the moment may pass without criticism. But now the anchor is heaved and the vessel sails to the west with a velocity equal to that at which the captain walks. In what direction does he now move, when he goes from stem to stern? You cannot say east, for the vessel is carrying him as fast towards the west as he walks to the east; and you cannot say west for the converse reason. In respect to surrounding space he is stationary, though to all on board the ship he seems to be moving. But now are we quite sure of this conclusion? Is he stationary? When we take into account the earth's motion around its axis,

_____
[1] Herbert Spencer's "First Principles," p. 54.

we find that instead of being stationary, he is
traveling at the rate of 1,000 miles per hour
to the east, so that neither the perception of
one who looks at him, nor the inference of one
who allows for the ship's motion is anything
like the truth.

"Nor indeed on further consideration shall
we find the revised conclusion to be much better,
for we have forgotten to allow for the earth's
motion in its orbit. This being some 68,000
miles per hour, it follows that, assuming the
time to be mid-day, he is moving not at the
rate of 1,000 miles per hour to the east, but
at the rate of 67,000 miles per hour to the
west. Nay, not even now have we discovered
the true rate and the true direction of his
movement. With the earth's progress in its
orbit, we have to join that of the solar system
towards the constellation Hercules, and when
we do this we perceive that he is moving
neither east nor west, but in a line inclined to
the plane of the ecliptic, and at a velocity
greater or less (according to the time of the
year) than that above named. To which let
us add that were the dynamic arrangements of
our sidereal system fully known to us, we should
probably discover the direction and rate of his
actual movement to differ considerably even
from these.

"How illusive are our ideas of motion is
thus made manifest; that which seems station-

ary proves to be moving; while that which we conclude to be going rapidly in one direction turns out to be going much more rapidly in the opposite direction. And so we are taught that what we are conscious of is not the real motion of any object, either in its rate or direction; but merely its motion as measured from an assigned position, either the position we ourselves occupy or some other."

There is no reason to suppose that the apparent motion of Mr. Spencer's ship varies more widely from its absolute motion than apparent truth to all finite minds varies from absolute truth; and what is the motion in the one case and the truth in the other, depends upon the standard by which each is determined.

That it is the motive of an act and not the act itself which determines its saving quality, is very distinctly stated in *Mark ix*. 38-50. John told Jesus that the disciples had caught someone casting out demons in his name, and they forbade him because he was not a follower with them of Jesus. But Jesus said: "Forbid him not, for there is no man who shall do a mighty work [or, exert a power] in my name, and be able quickly to speak evil of me. For he that is not against us is for us."

To do anything in the name of Jesus is to do it because, and only because it is presumed to be acceptable to Jesus. We can act from no higher motive. And however wide we may be from the perfect standard, what we shall have done will be acceptable to Him. "Whosoever," He adds, "shall give you a cup of cold water to drink, because ye are Christ's, verily I say unto you, he shall in no wise lose his reward." There is nothing in the giving of cold water but the motive for giving it that could insure His approbation.

With what propriety or justice, then, can any of us presume to prescribe a standard of truth for another, and to persecute or even reproach him for not accepting it, when our own standard is not only constantly changing but never absolutely corect?

"There probably is not one article in your creed or mine," says an eminent modern divine,[1] "that we shall read a thousand years hence as we do now, and it is a thing to make the angels laugh, were it not also so sad as to make them weep, the easy flippancy with which men still in the primer of God's wisdom pronounce themselves in theological finalities; set up a little Sinai for the arbitrament of doctrines *in perpetuum,* and incapable, as all men of course are, of letting their thoughts broaden out to the scope of God's truth, venture with conspicuous immodesty to constrain God's truth within the limitations of their thought."

Though two persons may be easily found to

---

[1] Sermon on "The Human Spirit and Divine Inspiration," by the Rev. Charles H. Parkhurst.

agree that a certain act or thought is right or true, good or false, yet no two ever have been or will be found to agree about the amount, degree or extent of that goodness or evil, of that truth or falsity; no two would exhibit precisely the same degree of persistence in the one case or resistance in the other; no two would make precisely the same degree of sacrifice in defending what they deemed good, or require the same amount of light or persuasion to surrender what they knew was wrong.

Truth is the containant of good. We cannot will to do good without putting it into some act or manifestation, as into a vessel. Such act or manifestation represents just so much truth as there is good contained or manifested in the execution of that specific volition. But we cannot supply these vessels of truth to others, because we cannot put into others a will to do good, from which will the vessels of truth are to be supplied. That must from the nature of the case be the voluntary and deliberate act of each individual. The power to control another's will would be fatal to its freedom. It is not what we profess, but what we believe and carry out into life that is truth to us, and if it is truth to us, there can be no harm in our believing it, while there is just as much harm in persecuting it out of us as if it were absolute truth.

Says Selden: " 'Tis a vain thing to talk of

a heretic, for a man from his heart can think
no otherwise than he does think."

Bishop Jeremy Taylor in his "Liberty of
Prophesying" says: "It is inconsistent with the
goodness of God to condemn those who err,
where the error hath nothing of the will in it,
who therefore cannot repent of the error because they believe it true. . . . For all have a
concomitant assent to the truth of what they
believe, and *no man can at the same time believe what he does not believe.*" [1]

It is only from this point of view that we can
discern and fully realize the wisdom and justice of the injunction given by our Saviour to
His disciples: "Judge not that ye be not
judged. For with what judgment ye judge, ye
shall be judged." When we judge another,
we necessarily judge by our own lights and
standards; our lights as to the facts, and our
own standard of duty, knowing little of his.
"For why," as Paul says, "is my liberty judged
by another's conscience?" Hence what we
commend or denounce might be good or bad
if done by us, but it by no means follows that
they would be similarly appreciated by infinite
wisdom. We, however, must be judged by our
judgment of others, for that is what is right

---

[1] Taylor wrote his "Liberty of Prophesying" while in
exile. When his church regained its ascendancy he
was not quite so fervent an apologist of the liberty
of prophesying.

or wrong in our eyes. To neglect the one,
therefore, or to do the other is to sin. Hence
it is that as we judge we shall be judged. In
judging others we are disclosing our own standards; we are seeing things by the only light
we have—but not with perfect light or with a
single eye. We may show how far we have
progressed in the knowledge of the true and
the good but we have no means of determining
how far our brother has advanced, still less
what enemies he has overcome.

> "Who made the heart, 'tis He alone
>   Decidedly can try us.
> He knows each chord—its various tone,
>   Each spring—its various bias.
>
> Then at the balance let's be mute,
>   We never can adjust it;
> What's done we partly may compute,
>   But know not what's resisted."

Jesus reproves the man who judges his
brother severely. "Thou hypocrite," He says,
"Cast out first the beam out of thine own eye;
and then thou shalt see clearly to cast out the
mote out of thy brother's eye." He does not
say that the hypocrite would see the mote more
clearly in his brother's eye from having removed the beam from his own eye, but only
that *he would see* more clearly to cast out the
mote from his brother's eye. He does not state
the process by which the mote is to be removed.

Why? Because all that he could accomplish in the way of the brother's reform must be accomplished by his first reforming himself. In proportion to his success in handling the beam in his own eye will the force of his example and the charm wrought in him by the change he has undergone in the struggle, stimulate the brother to similar efforts to be rid of his mote.

Faults to which in ourselves we are blind, we discern with singular acuteness in others; but when we attempt in dead earnest to correct these faults in ourselves, the faults we were so keen to discern in others shrink in their proportions to our eyes, quite as fast as our own do. We have no infallible standard by which to judge our brother's moral quality except by what we purpose and do ourselves. Says Isabella in "Measure for Measure,"

> "I have a brother is condemned to die;
> I do beseech you let it be his fault
> And not my brother."

Paul, the Apostle, who before his conversion had persecuted unto the death the followers of Christ, delivering into prison both men and women, when near the close of his apostolate he was brought before the Council said, "Men and brethren, I have lived in all good conscience before God until this day."

What does this mean except that he had acted upon the best lights he knew of, as well before as after he saw the great light which blinded him on his journey to Damascus; as well while persecuting Christians as afterwards while instructing them. Again in his first epistle to Timothy, Paul thanks Christ Jesus for appointing him to his service, "though," he says, "I was before a blasphemer and a persecutor and injurious: howbeit I obtained mercy because I did it ignorantly in unbelief."

In the Franco-Italian war, which resulted in driving the Austrians out of Italy, the curious spectacle was presented of an archbishop in France issuing a *Mandement* to the bishops and clergy of the empire to put up prayers in all the churches of his arch-episcopate for the success of the French arms, and of another archbishop of the same church in Austria issuing another *Mandement* to the bishops and other clergy in his arch-episcopate for the success of the Austrian arms. The emotions inspired by this spectacle in the breasts of those who were not directly under the intoxicating influences of this struggle are not incorrectly interpreted in the following extract from the diary of the late Crown Prince of Prussia:[1]

"After all it really is an irony on the Message of Salvation when each side prays to God for its own cause, as the righteous one, and at every success tries to prove that its opponent has been left in the lurch by Heaven."

[1] Crown Prince's Diary, p. 105.

And yet no one will doubt, certainly the Crown Prince himself would not have doubted, that there was quite as large a proportion in one of these armies as in the other who believed that they were combating for a cause that deserved the Divine blessing, and that their prayers were as well entitled to be heard as if they had prayed for any other earthly good or deliverance.

That genuine unity of the church based upon the indivisibility of truth on which Bossuet rested his indictment of Protestantism, is not the unity of man with men or with ecclesiastical corporations, as Bossuet imagined, but of man with Christ. Variations and divisions upon that point cannot be too much deplored, and if it had been of such variations that Bossuet had complained, his labors might have merited the fame they enjoyed.[1] But it was not the unity of man with Christ, but of man with the Church of Rome and the Church of Rome as

---

[1] But can hardly be said to enjoy any longer to the same extent as formerly. St. Marc Girardin, himself a devout Catholic, in a paper published a few years ago on Bossuet, said: "The fundamental idea of the *Histoire des Variations* is that the instability of opinions is the characteristic of error. Such was the prevailing idea in Bossuet's time. Today the variations of political liberty have taught us to be less severe. Our ancestors scarcely believed in the truth of doctrines if they were not invariable; in our day invincible tenacity of opinion seems to us equally one of the distinctive signs of error."

the exclusive proprietor of absolute matters of faith, for which he battled. He entirely misapprehended the nature and purpose of the institution, the foundations of which are laid in what Christians claim to be the Word of God, and which perhaps were never better defined than in the following striking passage from a letter of William Law:

"Religion or church communion, is in its true nature both external and internal, which are thus united and thus distinguished; the one is the *outward sign,* and the other is the *inward truth:* the one never was, nor ever can be, in its true state without the other. The inward truth or church is regeneration or the life, spirit and power of Christ, quickened and brought to life in the soul.

"The *outward sign,* or church is that outward *form* or manner of life that bears full witness to the truth of his regenerated life of Christ formed or revealed in the soul. The *inward truth* gives forth its proper outward manifestations of itself and these manifestations bring forth the true *outward church,* and make it to be *visible* and *outwardly* known.

"Thus everything in the inward life and spirit and will of Christ, when it becomes living, or inward man, is the *inward church* or kingdom of God set up within us: and everything in the *outward behavior* and visible conversation of Christ whilst dwelling among

42

men, when practised and followed by us in the
form and manner of our life, makes us the
members of that *outward church*, which He set
up in this world. Inwardly, nothing lived in
Christ but the sole will of God, a perpetual
regard to His glory and one continual desire
of the salvation of mankind. When this spirit
is in us, then we are inwardly one with Christ,
and united to God through Him. Outwardly,
Christ exercised every kind of love, kindness
and compassion to the souls and bodies of men;
nothing was visible in the outward form of his
life but humility and lowliness of state in every
shape; a contented want, or rather a total disregard of all worldly riches, power, ease or
pleasure; continual meekness, gentleness, patience, and resignation, not only to the will of
God, but to the haughty powers of the world,
to the perverseness and contradiction of all the
evil and malice of men and all the hardships
and trouble of human life. Now this and such
like *outward behavior* of Christ thus separated
from and contrary to the spirit, wisdom and
way of this world, was that very *outward
church* of which He willed all mankind to become visible and living members. And whoever in the spirit of Christ lives in the outward
exercise of these virtues, lives as to himself in
the highest perfection of *church* unity and is
the true inward and outward Christian. He is
all that he can be, he hath all he can have, he

doth all that he can do, and enjoyeth all that he can enjoy as a member of Christ's body or church in the world.

"For as Christ was God and man, come down from heaven for no other end but fully to restore the union that was lost between God and man, so church unity is and can be nothing else but the unity of this or that man or number of men with God, through the power and nature of Christ and therefore it must be the truth and the whole truth, that nothing more is required, nor will anything less be able to make anyone a true member of the Church of Christ, out of which there is no salvation, and in which there is no condemnation, but only and solely his conformity and union with the inward spirit and outward form of Christ's life and behavior in this world. This is the one fold under one shepherd, though the sheep are scattered or feeding in valleys, or on mountains ever so distant or separate from one another.

"On the other hand, not only every unreasonable, unjust action, be it done to whom it will, not only every unkind, proud, wrathful, scornful, disdainful, inward thought or outward behavior to any person, but every unreadiness to do good of all kinds to all that we can; every unwillingness to rejoice with them that rejoice, and to weep with them that weep, and to love our neighbor as ourselves; every aversion to be inwardly all love and outwardly all meekness, gentleness, courtesy and condescension in words and actions towards every creature for whom Christ died, makes us *Schismatics,* though we be ever so daily gathered together into one and the same place, joining in one and the same form of creed, prayers and praises offered to God, and is truly a *leaving* or *breaking* that *church unity* which makes us one with Christ as our Head, and unites us with men as the members of His body."

CHAPTER IV

THERE is danger of too much creed making. A creed, it is true, is to be judged, not by the interpretation that its architects or other ingenious minds may put upon it, but according to the meaning it will convey to those who repeat it. A creed that may seem perfectly true to some is liable to be wholly misapprehended by those who are less or more instructed. The endless dissensions provoked by the decrees of the Councils of Nice and Trent, by the Thirty-Nine Articles of the Anglican Church and by the Westminster Catechism, all still the torments of the Christian Church, are melancholy illustrations of this. A doctrinal statement of any kind, satisfactory to all, is and in this world always will be impossible; and to convey true doctrine to a people, it is really no paradox to say it must be differently presented to each man and woman.

More than half the population of the earth would reject the proposition that there is only one God, than which it would be difficult to frame a creed more universally acceptable to the civilized world, and yet even of those who accept it no two have precisely the same sort

46

of God in their minds. It is the diversity in our respective faculties for receiving truth which accounts for and begets the endless diversity of opinions among men and illustrates, not only the folly of expecting but the impossibility of securing entire conformity of faith between any two persons, to say nothing of a group or community of persons. Creeds are like fences, they keep more out of the church than they enclose, and the tendency to lengthen the creed and shorten the Decalogue is as much the vice of the Church to-day as it was in the days of Boileau. It is a species of persecution which keeps churches few where they should abound, empty where they should be thronged; paralyzes the clergy, degrades the ministerial office, and brings a reproach upon religion.

Christ came into the world to heal, not the well, but the sick; to bring, not the righteous, but sinners to repentance. "To whom little is forgiven, the same loveth little," are His words. The churches of Christendom have for the most part acted upon opposite principles in doing the most they could to drive from their communion those for whom Christ died and to whom His disciples were sent. There is as much wisdom as wit in a remark of D'Alembert, a century ago:

"As faith is a gift of God and not vouchsafed to all, religion may meet with unbelievers, but if it encounters enemies it is the fault of those who defend it with weapons which it reproves. It would be useful for this class of men to write the work of which a sage of our day has already provided the title: *'La Nécessité de Conversion des Dévots.'* "

Hence we have no need to believe a man, still less to proscribe him, when he denies the existence of a God or rejects the truths of the church. What he denies is only what he has been taught concerning God's existence and attributes and what he understands to be the doctrines of the church. Many a man has been ostracized by society as an atheist who had refused to believe, not in a God, but in the gods of some of his neighbors. Would the world, would France even, entertain more respect for Voltaire had he been always loyal to the church of which Louis XIV and Louis XV were the High Priests? Would he in that case ever have merited the eulogium bestowed upon him by Lecky of "having done more to destroy the greatest of human curses (persecution for opinion's sake) than any other of the sons of men," and can as precious an eulogium be pronounced over any one of the ministry, whether lay or clerical, of either of the sovereigns under whom he lived?

It is difficult to discern any moral difference between the man who persecutes or forces people into the church and one who persecutes or bribes people out of the church. Both may

act according to profound convictions and from
an equally strong desire to correct error and
propagate truth; but each makes the great
mistake of supposing that his is the only saving
creed and that any other is a gate to destruction. Horace Walpole, writing from Paris of
the *philosophes,* describes them as "insupportable, superficial, overbearing and fanatic."
"They preach incessantly," he says, "and their
doctrine is atheism; you would not believe how
openly. Don't wonder therefore if I should
return a Jesuit. Voltaire himself does not
satisfy them. One of their devotees said of
him, *'Il est bigot; c'est un déiste.'* Yet this
woman who denounced Voltaire as a bigot because he believed in a God was no doubt as
honest and as ready to go to the Bastille or the
stake for her opinions as Bossuet or Calvin."

It is our duty, whether as a church or as individuals to believe what we suppose to be the
best and highest truth and to impart it wherever we suppose we can do our neighbor good
by so doing. It is no concern of ours whether
he accepts all or any portion of our belief. We
may be wrong or he may be wrong, and we are
both certain to be more or less wrong. In
either case our teachings are not adapted to
his spiritual condition, or he would accept them.
We have done our whole duty in giving him
the opportunity to embrace them, and we have
no more right to quarrel with him for declining

our invitation than with a horse we have led to the pump, for declining to drink.

A truth not suited to our spiritual condition at the time would only be trampled under foot if offered us, and thus made unfit for our spiritual nourishment when, if ever, we should become qualified to assimilate it. Every religious dogma yet promulgated in the world has been heresy to a larger number than accepted it, while in every heresy there have been more or less important elements of truth.

It is not true, therefore, that a man should bear his testimony to what he regards as the highest truth without regard to time, place, seasons, or audience. He is to be governed by the same considerations in the use of his tongue as in everything else. He must try to do and say what he thinks best for his neighbor; not to approach him with his advice when it would prove a stumbling block, nor when it would tend to confirm him in his error, nor without a profound sense of his own liability to error.

"Let the Clazomaenians have leave to be immodest," was one clause of a decree proclaimed by the city of Athens in regard to some of the people of Clazomaene whose improprieties of behavior the laws of hospitality did not permit her to chastise. Christians should respect a law yet more venerable, and commended to our respect by a yet higher sanction, and that is the law of charíty, the chief of Christian virtues.

"We should remember those that are in bonds are bound with them," said Paul, and this is true whether they are bound in chains of steel or of theological delusions, whether they are immured in a felon's prison or in a debasing superstition.

"The true Christian," says the late Bishop Martensen, "does not belong to any particular sect. He may participate in the ceremonial service of every sect and still belong to none. He has only one science, which is Christ within him; he has only one desire, namely to do good. Look at the flowers of the field. Each one has its own particular attributes, nevertheless they do not wrangle and fight with each other. They do not quarrel about the possession of sunshine and rain or dispute about their colors. Each one grows according to its nature. Thus it is with the children of God. Each one has his own gifts and attributes, but they all spring from one spirit. They enjoy their gifts and praise the wisdom of Him from whom they originated. Why should they dispute about the qualities of Him whose attributes are manifest in themselves?

"We have all only one single order to which we belong, and the only rule of that order is to do the will of God, that is to say, to keep still and serve as instruments through which

God may do His will. Whatever God sows
and makes manifest in us, we give it back to
Him as His own fruit. The Kingdom of
Heaven is not based upon our opinions and
authorized beliefs, but rooted in its own Divine
power. Our main object ought to be to have
the Divine power within ourselves. If we
possess that, all scientific pursuit will be a mere
play of the intellectual faculties, with which to
amuse ourselves; for the true science is the
revelation of the wisdom of God within our
own minds.

"God manifests His wisdom through His
children, as the earth manifests her powers
through the production of various flowers and
fruits. Therefore let each one be glad of his
own gifts and enjoy those of others. Why
should all be alike? Who condemns the birds
of the forest because they do not all sing the
same tune, but each praises its Creator in its
own way? Nevertheless the power which enables them to sing, originates in all from only
one source." [1]

The same view is set forth with a more
philosophical precision by Swedenborg:

"Mutual love and charity are effective of
unity or oneness even amongst varieties, uniting
varieties into one; for let numbers be multiplied ever so much even to thousands and ten

---

[1] Quoted in Hartmann's "Life and Doctrine of Jacob
Boehm," p. 9.

thousands, if they are all principled in charity
or mutual love, they have all one end, *viz.,* the
common good, the Kingdom of the Lord and
the Lord Himself, in which case the varieties
of doctrine and worship are like the varieties
of the senses and viscera in man, as just observed, which contribute to the perfection of
the whole. For then the Lord by means of
charity enters into and operates upon all, with
a difference of manner according to the particular temper of each, and thus arranges all
and every one into order, as in heaven, so on
earth; and thus the will of the Lord is done on
earth as it is in heaven according to what He
Himself teaches." [1]

The errors of our ancestors counsel us to
be cautious in dogmatizing. Our own errors
counsel us to be still more cautious in condemn-
ing the dogmas of others.

When our Lord was journeying up to Jerusalem for the last time, it was convenient for
Him to pass through Samaria. The Samaritans
were not of the Israelitish race but were de-
scendants of those gentiles who had been sent
to people the land when the ten tribes were
carried away. Though to some extent idolaters, they had set up a worship of Jehovah as
"the God of the land," and in the course of
time this worship had prevailed to such an
extent as to awaken the jealousy of the Jews,

---

[1] *Arcana Coelestia,* n. 1285.

who selfishly disputed their right to be numbered among the chosen people. So strong was this feeling in our Lord's time that, in reply to a remark which He made to a Samaritan woman from whom He asked a cup of water, she said, "The Jews have no dealings with the Samaritans."

On the occasion of the final visit to Jerusalem to which we have referred, messengers went before Him to prepare a resting place for Him at the close of each day's journey. At one Samaritan village through which He had proposed to pass, the people refused the privileges and the reason assigned by them was such as might be expected from the strained relations existing between this people and the Jews: "because His face was as though He would go to Jerusalem."

When this answer was brought back, James and John were highly indignant and said, "Lord, wilt thou that we command fire to come down and consume them, even as Elijah did?"

This was a very natural suggestion and substantially what everyone does who proscribes a man or sect for their opinions or presumes to sit in judgment upon another's moral condition. And it is instructive to note that John the beloved disciple, who only a few days later was permitted to lay his head affectionately upon the Lord's breast, was one of the two from whom this cruel proposal came. But what was the

Lord's reply? "He turned and rebuked them saying, Ye know not what manner of Spirit ye are of." The result was that, instead of burning up these inhospitable Samaritans, "they went to another village."

How large a portion of the world behaves as these Samaritans did when Christ comes to them, with His face "as though He would go to Jerusalem," and not to their church, and how many of the professed followers of Jesus are ready like James and John to invoke Divine wrath upon them for their inhospitable exclusion, merely because they too "know not what manner of spirit they are of." Jesus not only did not visit with His wrath this village which acted according to its lights; nor did He judge other Samaritans harshly because of the treatment He had received from some of them; but He passed on to another Samaritan village, trusting to the chance of finding there toleration at least, if not a welcome.

The secret of this trust was not known to His companions, for they "knew not what manner of spirit they were of;" still less what manner of spirit these Samaritans were of. A few days later the Lord had an experience which enables us to discern the secret of this trust and helps to explain the gentleness of His dealing with the villagers who refused Him passage through their territory. The story is thus told by *Luke* (*xvii.* 11-19):

"And it came to pass as they were on the way to Jerusalem that he was passing through Samaria and Galilee. And as he entered into a certain village, there met him ten men that were lepers, which stood afar off; and they lifted up their voices, saying, Jesus, Master, have mercy on us. And when he saw them, he said unto them, Go and show yourselves unto the priests. And it came to pass, as they went they were cleansed. And one of them, when he saw that he was healed, turned back, with a loud voice glorifying God; and he fell upon his face at his feet, giving him thanks: and he was a Samaritan. And Jesus answering said, Were not the ten cleansed? but where are the nine? Were there none found that returned to give glory to God, save this stranger? And he said unto him, Arise, and go thy way: thy faith hath made thee whole."

If these incidents so dramatically told by the Apostle teach any one lesson more distinctly than another, it is that our war should be with sin rather than with sinners; with our own sinfulness rather than with that of our neighbors.

On this same journey, and probably on the same day, Jesus related the parable of the two men who went up into the Temple to pray, the one a Pharisee and the other a publican. This parable, Luke tells us [1] "was spoken unto certain which trusted in themselves that they were

---

[1] *Chap. xviii.* 9.

righteous and set all others at nought"; in other words to the class within which has originated all the persecution for opinion's sake which has tormented our race since the foundations of the earth were laid.

The positive philosophy of Comte was very far from embodying the whole teaching of Christ, and yet it has unquestionably given a holy dignity and comfort to multitudes whom the Bible failed to quicken into spiritual life. Of this, Littré, the illustrious French lexicographer, was a typical illustration.

"I resign myself," he said in his last illness, "to the inexorable laws of nature. The positive philosophy which has done so much to sustain me during the past thirty years and which, by giving me an ideal, a thirst for the better, the light of history, solicitude for humanity, has saved me from being a simple negator, and has stood by me faithfully in my recent trial."

Only about a year before his death Littré pronounced Catholicism "the natural enemy of all freedom," but, said Rénan after quoting the remark, "tolerant for the intolerant, he insisted upon the faithful application of abstract principles. He was convinced that the tolerant would possess the earth and that the liberalism which has no fear of the liberty of others, wears the seal of truth."

While on a visit to a lighthouse on the coast of Brittany in 1872, he fell from the first story and sustained some bruises in consequence. A journalist of the neighborhood expressed regret that he had not broken his neck. "We did not think alike on theological questions," Littré added in telling the story. That was all the rebuke he had for the uncharitable journalist.

Divine truth has been aptly compared to the pure light of heaven, while man's conception of it is like his shadow upon the wall, a form of the light but diminished in intensity and shaped in outline to each individual's proportions and receptivity.

"The times of ignorance," Paul tells us, "God winked at." Those times have not ceased. They will never cease. There are none of us who could hope for salvation if our ignorance were not mercifully winked at. But if the Master mercifully winks at our ignorance, can we do better than wink at one another's ignorance? Can we ask our ignorance to be winked at if we refuse to wink at the ignorance of our neighbor?

The Lord tolerated polygamy among the Jews; why should we persecute it among the Mahommedans, to whom it seems to be quite as permissible as it ever was to the Children of Israel? The true church must necessarily be adapted to the lowest as well as to the highest states of spiritual intelligence, and able to accommodate its truths to the extremes of

58

ignorance, brutality, and selfishness. If God be, as we are assured, the same yesterday, to-day, and forever, we may not doubt that all the religions that have prevailed or that now prevail upon the earth, have a place in accomplishing the purposes of the Divine Wisdom.

CHAPTER V

THERE is no one who does not from time to time break every one of the commandments. "Whosoever," says the apostle James, "shall keep the whole and yet offend in one point, he is guilty of all."

We may not literally commit the crimes of murder, adultery, theft, etc., as defined by our civil law, but every one of us yields to impulses occasionally which have in them the rudiments of all those crimes and lack only the opportunity and temptation and exemption from legal penalties to lead to commission of them.

With what propriety or justice, then, can we turn in wrath upon those who incur the civil penalties for these crimes because of the form in which they were committed, and withhold from them our charity and love? Our Master never withholds His. It was not by accident that Jesus after His crucifixion first appeared to that one of all his followers out of whom He had cast seven devils.

The desire to have others agree with us in opinion is more frequently due to our self-love, our vanity, our desire to rule, to have

60

our own way—in other words, to the impulses of an unregenerate and selfish nature—than to a concern for the welfare of those who differ with us. Hence it is that most of the dissensions, jealousies, controversies and persecutions, not only of individuals but of bodies social, political and ecclesiastical have had their origin in this desire to make others surrender their own opinions to ours; to cease to be themselves and pretend to be what they are not. It is only as we put off the natural man and our spiritual perceptions are opened, that we cease to be unhappy when others disagree with us; that we begin to feel the same solicitude for the freedom of others that we have for our own.

The diversity in the constituents of our natural bodies is infinite. What resemblance is there between the bone, the flesh, the hair, the nerves, or between their respective functions? Infinite as is their variety, they never have been precisely the same in any two individuals, yet all are necessary for the perfection of an earthly dwelling-place for our souls. If nature be what it is difficult to see how anyone can doubt it is—the thought of God expressed in language intelligible to finite beings —why should we expect less diversity of organs and functions in the constituents of the spiritual bodies of which society and the church are composed, than in the natural?

Swedenborg has a pregnant sentence on this subject. In his *Arcana Coelestia,* n. 3451, he says:

"With respect to the Lord's kingdom in the earth, that is, with respect to his Church, the case is this, that whereas it derives its doctrinals from the literal sense of the Word, it must needs be various and diverse as to these doctrinals. One society will profess one thing to be a truth of faith because it is so said in the Word; another society will profess another thing because it is also so said. Consequently the Church of the Lord, inasmuch as it derives its doctrinals from the literal sense of the Word, will differ in every different place, and this not only according to societies, but sometimes according to particular persons in each society. Nevertheless a difference in doctrinals of faith does not cause the Church not to be one, provided only there be unanimity as to willing well and doing what is good."

Christ forebore to condemn the woman taken in adultery; not because she had not sinned, for he told her to go and sin no more, but because all her accusers from the eldest unto the last, in other words, all her fellow creatures had been as flagrant sinners as she, if not in the same, in other ways.

Unity in religion can only be secured at the expense of truth. We could have unity if all would think as we do, but no one can think as we do without thinking differently from many others and differently from the way we may think tomorrow. The Latin church professes to believe that Providence has secured to it that unity which can only result from absolute certainty, by making its clergy the infallible interpreters of revealed truth. But this unity is only attainable at the expense of the reason, for necessarily in such a case it is only the hierarchy who can be permitted to exercise their reason. But the reason is the faculty by which we test all truth, and if we do not exercise it we cannot distinguish the authority of the Bible from the authority of any other book; nor can we determine the claims of any ecclesiastical hierarchy to our respect. There is no escaping the fact that ecclesiastical unity is moral idiocy.

> Sure, He that made us with such large discourse,
> Looking before and after, gave us not
> The capability and Godlike reason
> To rust in us unus'd.

And in confirmation of this it may be observed that the more fanatical about its religion a people is, the lower will all its moral standards be found to be, and the less does it feel or know of love to the neighbor—the crucial test of a religious character.

"Go thy way," said Jesus to the centurion, "as thou hast believed"—not as your priest or bishop has believed—"be it done unto thee."

When we denounce or persecute a man for having opinions different from our own; for what to us seems heresy, we practically accuse him of robbing us of a portion of our share of truth in the world, and leaving error in its place. This is of course a delusion. A man might preach till doomsday the once prevailing theory that the sun revolved around the earth, or that the earth rested on the back of a tortoise, but the truth in regard to the relations of the sun and the earth would not be affected in the least by these fancies.

Hence it is, we confidently believe, that the so called variations of Protestantism, not its dogmas, are its chief elements of strength, and the dogmatic unity and professed immutability of the Latin church its fatal element of weakness.

In judging, denouncing, and, if in our power, persecuting others, how rarely it occurs to us that we are ourselves all sinners and equally exposed to persecution with our victims; that "there is none that doeth good, no not one," and that the sin or evil we denounce in another is only an aspect of his conduct as seen by us from a plane of spiritual development really or supposed to be a little more advanced than his. The act, thus viewed from the higher plane, seems sinful, but no more so than our own conduct will seem to those dwelling upon a yet higher spiritual plane, whose conduct will in turn similarly impress those who occupy a plane still higher, and so on *ad infinitum*.

"It is a known thing," says one whom I am disposed to regard as the profoundest of ethical philosophers, whether living or dead, "that man is born into the nature of his parents, and of his grandfathers, and also of his great-grandfathers, in a long succession of ages; consequently he is born into the hereditary evil of them all successively accumulated, insomuch that as to what is from himself he is nothing but evil. Hence has come this further consequence, that both as to understanding and as to will he is altogether ruined, and of himself wills nothing of good, and thence understands nothing of truth, consequently, that what he calls good, yea, believes to be good, is evil, and what he calls truth, yea, believes to be truth, is false; as for example, to love himself better than others, to be better disposed towards himself than towards others, to desire what belongs to another, and to be concerned and studious about himself, and not about others except for the sake of himself. Inasmuch as of himself he is inclined to these things, therefore he calls them good, and also true; and further, if anyone injures or endeavors to injure him as to these goods and truths, as he calls them, he hates such a person, and also burns with revenge towards him, desiring and likewise meditating his ruin, wherein he perceives delight, and this in proportion as he actually confirms himself in the above dispositions, that is, in proportion as he more frequently brings them into exercise by act. Such an one, when he comes into another life, has the same desires, the essential nature remaining which he has contracted in the world by actual life, and the essential delight thereof being manifestly perceived; wherefore he cannot be in any heavenly society, in which everyone wishes better to others than to himself, but in some infernal society, which enjoys the same delight as himself. This nature is what ought to be extirpated during man's life in the world, which can be effected only by regeneration from the Lord, that is, by receiving altogether another will, and thence another understanding; or, in other words, by being made new as to both of these faculties. But, for this purpose, he must needs first of all be reborn as an infant, and learn what is evil and false, and also what is good and true, for without science or knowledge he cannot imbibe any good, inasmuch as of himself he acknowledges nothing to be good but what is evil, and nothing to be true but what is false. With this view, such knowledges are insinuated into him as are not altogether contrary to those which he before had, as that all love begins from self, that self is first to be regarded and then others,

66

that good is to be done to such as appear poor and miserable in an external form, whatsoever may be their inward qualities; in like manner, that widows and orphans, on account of their name only, are objects of charity; and lastly, that enemies in general, whosoever they may be, are like objects; and by doing good to such, man may merit heaven. These and similar knowledges are those of the infancy of his new life, and are such as, deriving somewhat from his former life or the nature of his former life, derive somewhat also from his new life, into which he is thus introduced; and hence they are such as to admit in them whatsoever things are conducive towards forming the new will and the new understanding. These are the lowest goods and truths, from which the regenrate life commences, and inasmuch as they are admissive of interior truths, or such as are nearer to Divine, false principles may be thereby extirpated, which before had been belived to be true.[1]

---

[1] Swedenborg's *Arcana Coelestia*, n. 3701.

THE UNFAILING MORAL
STANDARD

THE UNFAILING MORAL
STANDARD

CHAPTER I

EVERYONE has a standard by which he determines for himself what is right and what
is wrong. No race of men has yet been discovered, nor is there a plausible reason for
supposing there ever existed any individual or
any race of human beings so rude and degraded
as to lack entirely the faculty of distinguishing
between what they regarded as good and what
they regarded as evil; what they regarded as
true, and what false; what they regarded as
right, and what wrong.

While every being created in God's image
has notions of what he deems right and wrong,
it does not follow that any two will commend
or denounce precisely the same act, or, if they
should, that they would commend or denounce
any particular act for precisely the same reason
or in precisely the same degree; still less that
either will ever rise to the comprehension of
the absolute good or the absolute evil. When
we speak of a man's good or evil acts, we judge
his conduct either by his standard or by our
own. No one of us can ever pretend to know

what is right or wrong according to the standards of Infinite Wisdom. Is there, then, any universal standard that all will accept? Yes, and no! Paradoxical as it may appear, there is one standard which all will recognize, and yet the standards of no two persons are ever entirely the same.

The only standard of duty common to all people is to be found in the universal recognition of the propriety of doing unto others as we would that others, under precisely like circumstances, should do unto us, and of doing nothing unto others which, under precisely similar circumstances, we should not wish done unto us. There are sections of the human family who have what appear to be other, or at least supplementary standards from which they take no appeal. A considerable portion of the civilized world accepts the Bible, or parts of it at least, as defining the highest standard of duty; another considerable portion looks to the writings of Confucius for its moral guidance; still larger numbers to the Koran of Mahomet, and other considerable portions to the teachings of Buddha and of Brahma. The Mormon Bible is also a final standard with some, but it is safe to say that no two persons attach precisely the same importance or the same significance to any of these codes, while it is not possible to conceive of a rational person, be he Jew or Gentile, saint or savage,

72

bond or free, contesting the Golden Rule as a standard by which to judge the conduct of his fellow creatures, however careless he may be about living up to that standard himself.

It is by this standard that we measure man's progress from the animal to what we are accustomed to term the civilized state. In fact, it is only by this standard that civilization can be accurately measured. As the Golden Rule becomes the rule of life, man becomes increasingly gracious, social, trustful, considerate of the interests and welfare of his fellow creatures and proportionately dependent upon them.

The most striking feature of human society in Christian countries is the rapid consolidation of interests which has marked its progress; the inter-dependence, not only of separate nationalities, but of communities within those nationalities, which the advance in science and the arts has made not only practicable but necessary. The number of separate states or political sovereignties has been as steadily diminishing, while the facilities of intercourse have been as constantly on the increase.

A standard of duty which is universal must know none of the limitations of time or space. There is no reason to suppose that the Golden Rule has ever been subject to any such limitations; no one ever reached the age of rationality without knowing how he would like to be treated by others, and to know that is to be conscious of a duty to treat one's neighbors as well.

This rule of life was in the beginning. It was old when Moses brought down from the Mount for the Jews the two tables of stone, on which was the first formal inscription of this universal law of which we have any knowledge—the first table setting forth man's duties to God and the second his duties to his fellow man, his neighbor. These latter duties will be found specifically elaborated in *Leviticus,* where the Lord is reported to have said to Moses:

"Speak unto all the children of Israel and say unto them: . . . . Ye shall do no unrighteousness in judgment: thou shalt not respect the person of the poor, nor honor the person of the mighty: but in righteousness shalt thou judge thy neighbor. Thou shalt not go up and down as a talebearer among thy people; neither shalt thou stand against the blood of thy neighbor: I am the Lord. Thou shalt not hate thy brother in thine heart: thou shalt surely rebuke thy neighbor, and not bear sin because of him. Thou shalt not take vengeance or bear any grudge against the children of thy people: *but thou shalt love thy neighbor as thyself: I am the Lord.*"

Jesus gave His disciples an abstract of all these directions in a more compendious form in His reply to a Pharisee of the legal profession who thought to compromise Him by asking

Him, "Which is the great commandment in
the law?" (*Matt. xxii.* 37.) Jesus replied:
"Thou shalt love the Lord thy God with all
thy heart, and with all thy soul, and with all
thy mind. This is the first and great commandment. And the second is like unto it,
Thou shalt love thy neighbor as thyself. On
these two commandments hang all the law and
the prophets."

This second great commandment is reported
in a yet more compact form in *Matthew vii.*
12 in these words:

"Therefore all things whatsoever ye would
that men should do to you, do ye even so to
them; for this is the law and the prophets."

It is given as follows in *Luke vi.* 31: "And
as ye would that men should do to you, do ye
also to them likewise. For if ye love them
which love you, what thank have ye? for sinners also do even the same."

There is a distinction made here in the loves
we are to cultivate which many devout Christians are prone to lose sight of. We are com-
manded to love the Lord our God with all
our heart and soul and mind, but we are to
love our neighbor only as ourselves. It has
been in all ages but too common a notion that
if it is a good thing to love our neighbor as
ourselves, the more we love him better than
ourselves, so much the better person we shall
deserve to be esteemed. There is apt to be a
conceit in this putting ourselves last; in ever

75

trying to appear outwardly and externally laying down our lives. To make one's self last outwardly in order to make one's self first spiritually is just as unjust and selfish as to insist on being made first for whatever earthly glory there might be to that position. Others have as much right to this distinction of being last as we have.

An ambition to excel our neighbors in heavenliness is even more satanic than to strive to excel them in wealth, in worldly power and position. If we avoid taking positions of prominence in the world because they are liable to stimulate worldly pride, we have no right to subject one of our neighbors to such temptations. If in our manners we seem to love our neighbor more than we love ourselves, beside cultivating in ourselves the conceits of self-righteousness, we wrong our neighbor by depriving him of the privilege of being the last and the most self-effacing himself. The struggle to be first is the expression of earthly pride; the struggle to be last is the expression of self-righteous conceit. To love yourself as you love others is the proper observance of the Divine law of love to the neighbor. There is always more or less worldly pride lurking in efforts to wear the garb and countenance of exceptional humility, while there can be no conceit in claiming no spiritual superiority over our neighbors.

CHAPTER II

THERE is a disposition in all of us to entertain an exaggerated sense of responsibility for
the consequences of what we do or leave un-
done, and of individual importance in carrying
on the affairs of creation. Not content with
simply doing our duty as we understand it and
leaving it to the Lord to fashion results, we
worry when things do not go as we think they
should, and denounce ourselves or our asso-
ciates for not having done more or otherwise
than we or they have done. We fancy our
country is going to destruction when our party
or our views do not prevail, and sigh for the
sagacious, the patriotic, the holy men of whom
death has bereaved us, or for a form of government that seems to us better suited to the
needs of our people and time, despairing of
the Lord's power to bring order out of con-
fusion, the welfare of the many out of the
selfishness of all; and entirely overlooking the
need of the providential abuses we deplore.
Much of our solicitude about our family, about
the education, training and associations of our
children, about the health and worldly provision for the welfare of our kindred, friends,

neighbors, and country, is more or less infected with this delusion in regard to our individual power and importance.

The exercise of those affections or motives which are in harmony with Divine order will constrain us to do what we think best calculated to promote the happiness and welfare of our family, friends, country, etc., while the indulgence of those affections which are in conflict with Divine order will dispose us to subordinate the welfare of family, friends and country to our own; to disregard the law which requires us to do unto others as we would have them do unto us, and instead, to try to become a law unto ourselves.

It is a universal law that, whatever a man tries to do to another, whether it be good or evil, liberal or selfish, precisely such are the things which return in their fullest effects upon him. The exercise of love and charity toward others surrounds us with a sphere of influences proportioned to our own spiritual growth and stature, but God mercifully leaves no one dependent upon the love or wisdom of any other mortal. If He did, what a fearful fate would await the millions who are growing up under the contaminating influences of vice in its most hideous developments with a very imperfect apprehension of its dangers! How dreadful to contemplate the destiny of all children if left to the mercy of mere human wisdom and affection! For who is competent alone to train a child, when we all require God's infinite grace continually to protect us from the natural consequences of our own proclivity to evil? The whole business and duty of life consists in rejecting all improper and selfish motives of action and selecting none but such as are animated by love to God and charity to our neighbor.

The events of life, and even its duration, should be left entirely and without solicitude to Providence. It is only the unregenerate and sinful part of our being that ever comes into jeopardy; it is only the selfish desires with their affections that are allowed to suffer harm. The Divine sphere of protection flows out and encompasses everything good and true that is implanted within us. Not one drop of heavenly oil, not one drop of heavenly wine can be reached by the evil or suffer hurt. No single affection of good and no genuine wisdom can ever be lost. Not one element or constituent of the spiritual life, not a single regenerated principle of the mind will ever decay.

Paul uttered a universal truth when he said to the Hebrews: "The Lord is my helper, and I will not fear what man shall do unto me." The Lord is as much a helper to all the children of men to-day as he ever was to Paul.

Paul in his letter to the Galatians said: "Use not your freedom for an occasion to the flesh, but through love; be servants one to another; even as this; thou shalt love thy neighbour as thyself; but if ye bite and devour one another, take heed that ye be not consumed one of another."

It is the instinct, born within us, which lets us know how we should treat others by leaving us never in ignorance of the way we wish to be treated under like circumstances ourselves, that constitutes what is technically described as Conscience, and differentiates its lessons from those derived exclusively from the Bible or Divine Revelation. It was clearly the Golden Rule to which Paul referred when in his letter to the Romans he wrote:

"For not the hearers of the law are righteous before God, but the doers of the law shall be justified, for when Gentiles which have no law, do by nature the things of the law, these, having no law, are a law unto themselves in that they show the work of the law written in their hearts; *their conscience bearing witness therewith,* and their thoughts, one with another, accusing or else excusing them, in the day when God shall judge the secrets of men according to my gospel by Jesus Christ."

Here Paul uses the word conscience as a witness of the law written in the hearts of the Gentiles; that is, of the people to whom the religion of the Bible had not been revealed;

who have no law, and do by nature the things of the law.

It was that conscience also that Paul found among the Athenians, and to which he refers in his famous address in the Areopagus at Athens, when he says, "Ye men of Athens, in all things I perceive that ye are somewhat religious.[1] For as I passed along and observed the objects of your worship, I found also an altar with this inscription, To the unknown God. What therefore ye worship in ignorance, this set I forth unto you."

Manifestly it was not superstitions that Paul proposed to set forth and commend to them, but what they worshipped in ignorance. They had the Golden Rule, but they had not, nor did any of the Gentiles have, what Paul proceeded to expound to them; any "knowledge of the one God that made the world and all things therein, he being Lord of heaven and earth; who, unlike the images they worshipped for God, did not dwell in temples made with hands, nor was served by men's hands as though he needed anything, seeing he giveth to all life, and breath, and all things; that made of one blood every nation that they should seek God if haply they might feel after him and find him;

---

[1] (Revised Version, marg. note, *Acts xvii. 22.*) In the text the word "superstitious" is used, though "religious" is manifestly better.

that he is not far from each one of us, on the contrary that in him we live and move and have our being. For we are also his offspring, and being the offspring of God, we ought not to think that the Godhead is like unto gold or silver, or stone graven by art and device of man."

All these things were new to the Athenians. The Golden Rule did not teach them, though teaching nothing in conflict with them. Hence Paul goes on: "The times of ignorance therefore God overlooked."

So the conscience teaches everyone his duties to his neighbor, so far as they may be taught without revelation. It is this consciousness, ever active in every human heart—which informs us how we ought to conduct ourselves towards others by never letting us forget how we would like others to conduct themselves towards us—which gives such weight to these words of the prophet Malachi:

"From the rising of the sun unto the going down of the same my name is great among the Gentiles, and in every place incense is offered unto my name and a pure offering, for my name is great among the Gentiles, saith the Lord of Hosts." [1]

The Gentiles or heathen, of course, knew nothing of religion as revealed to the Jews. God's name was great among them and in-

----

[1] *Malachi i. 2.*

cense was offered to that name simply by their constitutional ability to know how others should be treated, through knowing how they would like to be treated themselves.

So when Jesus was teaching in the Temple and the chief priests and elders sought to embarrass him with questions, He said, "Verily I say unto you, that the publicans and the harlots go into the kingdom of God before you." And that not in virtue of any teaching from Jesus or His disciples, but through that inner light bestowed upon all, and of which no one while in this world is wholly bereaved.

CHAPTER III

ONE of the Roman Emperors is reported to have had the negative or prohibitory form of the Golden Rule written conspicuously in letters of gold on the walls of his palace: *Quod tibi fieri non vis, alteri ne faceris.*[1] Confucius had presented it to the world in the same form many centuries before Romulus and Remus had been heard of.

It is a wonderful provision of Divine Providence that our natural selfishness, which is always an attempt to usurp or appropiate to ourselves the attributes of God, and which it is the great purpose of our creation and training in this world to extirpate, should be one of the most important agencies to make us constantly aware of our duty to our neighbor.

The instant anything in our lives disturbs, disappoints, annoys, vexes, offends or afflicts us, we know whether under the like circumstances the same thing would disturb, disappoint, annoy, vex, offend or afflict not only one but every one of our fellow creatures. That consciousness, or conscience, is our constant, our

[1] What you would not wish done to yourself, do not to another.

84

inseparable companion. This is an ethical school in which everyone is a pupil all his life.

It is an equally marvelous provision of Providence that, just so fast and so far as we overcome the selfishness or selfhood which is born in us, and acquire the habit of doing to others as we would have others do to us, just so fast and so far we are warranted in expecting that the visits of these messengers of discomfort, mercifully sent to warn us of our duties to one another and the peril of neglecting them, will become less frequent because less necessary.

Our natural selfishness will always incline us to extenuate or be unconscious of wrongs we may have done or may be doing to another, but when we witness the same act done to ourselves, or even to others by others, we are apt to swell with sudden resentment. Do we not constantly hear almost every social and political vice denounced in unmeasured terms by people who are unconsciously more or less guilty of them all? Who more prompt to rebuke in others their social and political aspirations, their lusts of wealth or power than those who share them most? The disciples of Jesus rebuked the mothers who brought their children to be touched by Jesus. When Zebedee's wife asked Jesus that her two sons might sit, one on His right hand and one on His left in his kingdom, the ten when they heard of it were indignant. Jesus, however, shared neither their jealousy nor their indignation.

So we all hunt foxes that steal our poultry, wolves that eat our sheep, yet we exhibit the same disregard of life in satisfying our appetite as they, and out of our abundance how rarely do we think of providing for the satisfaction of their appetites excepting the better to prepare them for the gratification of our own.

When King David was told of a rich man who, to entertain a guest, had violently appropriated a ewe lamb of one of his poor neighbors instead of taking one from his own flock, he was filled with indignation. "As the Lord liveth," he exclaimed, never suspecting he was judging himself, "the man that hath done this is worthy of death." When the prophet said to him, "Thou art the man," the King did not defend himself. By that light which is never extinguished within us, he saw his guilt and confessed: "I have sinned against the Lord." [1]

However irregular the life we lead ourselves, we are apt to judge others by our highest standards, and ourselves by the lowest. So we expect others to treat us according to our highest standards, but if they treat us according to our lowest standards—that being, perhaps, the way we treat them—we are apt to feel wounded, if not indignant. We speak freely of what we esteem—correctly, perhaps

[1] *II Samuel, xii.* 5.

—the faults or weaknesses of our friend. Should we hear of his taking a similar liberty with us, we are sure to feel surprised and wronged, and a coolness, if not a rupture of social relations, ensues. The laws of civil society against slander and libel and the judicial decisions for their construction are but a confirmation and amplification of this view.

Professor Sidgwick in his "Methods of Ethics," referring to the Golden Rule as formulated by Jesus, says: "This formula is obviously unprecise in statement; for one might wish for another's co-operation in sin and be willing to reciprocate it. Nor is it even true to say that we ought to do to others only what we think is right for them to do to us, for no one will deny that there may be differences in the circumstances—and even in the natures—of two individuals, A and B, in the way in which it is right for B to treat A."

It is but fair to Professor Sidgwick to say that he was scarcely at his best in the criticism here quoted. He pronounces the Golden Rule unprecise because "one might wish for another's co-operation in sin and be willing to reciprocate it." But no one is willing to co-operate with another in sinning against himself. To be willing to co-operate in sinning against a third person is not the equivalent of wishing the co-operator to sin in the like or in any other way against one's self.

It is impossible to conceive of a person wronging another if he knew that he himself was to be wronged and to suffer simultaneously and to precisely the same extent. The obligation to do unto others as we would have them do unto us does not carry with it any implication that a person wishing to act in obedience to it would take precisely the same view of his duty as everybody else, or indeed, as anyone else would take of it. On the contrary, it is of the first importance to recognize as inexorable laws of ethical science:

First, that every man's standard of right and wrong is as liable to differ from every other man's, as his age, education, temperament, health, and environment have differed.

Every man's God is his highest ideal. When we pray that His name be hallowed, by "name" we understand and have in our minds a Being endowed with such attributes as our highest ideal of existence can invest Him with. But as no two men's ideals are the same, so no two men have ever worshipped precisely the same God. It is equally true that no one person worships the same God for any considerable time. His God necessarily changes with his ideals, and his ideals change the more or less as he strives to apprehend the attributes of God, which can neither be counted nor measured. Of course there must be a corresponding diversity in men's notions of right and wrong.[1]

When at Lystra, Paul the Apostle caused one who had been a cripple from his mother's womb to leap up and walk, the multitude who witnessed it exclaimed: "The gods are come down to us, in the likeness of men;" and they called Barnabas, Jupiter, and Paul, Mercury, because he was the chief speaker, and the priest of Jupiter prepared oxen and garlands to offer sacrifices unto them.[2]

Second, the essential moral quality of every act of our lives must depend upon the motives or intention which inspired it. So far as that motive is in accord with the supreme and universal law to which I have referred, it deserves to be called a good act so far as its author was concerned. In so far as it was in conflict with this law, it would deserve to be called a bad act so far as its author is concerned, quite irrespective of the physical or phenomenal results of the act itself. The Christ is ever saying to all of us as he said to the Centurion,

---

[1] "All ideas and feelings are religious which refer to an ideal existence that fully corresponds to the wishes and requirements of the human mind." (Wundt's "The Facts of a Moral Life," p. 59.) Ludwig Feuerback sums up this view of religion in the short formula: "The gods are realizations in thought of the wishes of men."

[2] *Acts xiv.* 9.

"Go thy way; as thou hast believed, so be it done unto thee." [1]

---

[1] Swedenborg professes to have found confirmation of this view of moral responsibility in the spiritual world. He says:

"There are two things which make the life of man, will and understanding, and all things which are done by man are done by his will and by his understanding. Without these agents man would not have any action or speech other than a machine. Thence it is manifest that man is such a man as his will and understanding; and also that the action of man in itself is such as is the affection of his will that produces it .... Wherefore many men may speak and act alike, and yet they act and speak differently, one from a perverse will and thought, and the other from an upright will and thought. . . . In the spiritual world I have met with many who in the natural world have lived like others, by clothing themselves splendidly, feasting sumptuously, trading with borrowed money as others, seeing stage-plays, joking upon amatory matters as if from lust, besides other like things, and yet the angels charged these things upon some as evils of sin, and to some they did not impute them as evils; and the latter they declared innocent, but the former guilty. To the question why they did so when they had done things alike, the angels replied that they contemplate all from the purpose, intention or end, and distinguish according to them. Those, therefore, whom the end excuses or condemns, they excuse or condemn." (*Conjugial Love*, n. 527.)

CHAPTER IV

As the fear of the Lord is the beginning of wisdom, so the recognition of the distinction between real and apparent, between primary and secondary motives, lies at the foundation of Ethical Science. When Judas kissed Jesus in the Garden, his apparent motive was to testify or be deemed to testify affection for his Master. The less apparent motive was to betray Jesus to those who sought His life. A motive still less obvious and to which the others were doubtless all subordinate was to earn the stipulated reward of his infidelity. But the real or final motive of the act which will perpetuate his name as long, at least, as that of any of the disciples of Jesus lay, no doubt, far behind his thirst for money and could only be discerned by Supreme Intelligence. All we are certain of is that his treachery must have had its origin in a good or a bad motive; must have been inspired by a righteous or a wicked intent, for one or the other of these motives is the soul which inhabits every act and thought of our lives.

In the eyes of some, St. Peter's Church at Rome represents the taste and skill of its architects; these and nothing more. In a higher sense, it represents the devotion, self-denial and piety of some, the vanity and ambition of others. The money, genius and labor employed in its construction may have been contributed by one class for the love of God, by another through fear of ecclesiastical censure, and by yet another to increase the commercial value of adjacent property or to gratify municipal pride; and by some from yet meaner motives. The final motive, as referred to in these pages, is the *essential* motive, force or impulse, and always involves an election, consciously or unconsciously, to do what shall seem according to our standards at the time right or wrong.

Every act of our lives is a link in a chain of motives having one end in the spiritual, which is the real world, and the other in the natural or apparent world, upon which, as on a ladder, angels good or bad are ever ascending and descending. "When the second causes which are next unto the senses," says Lord Bacon, "do offer themselves to the mind of man, if it stay and dwell there, it may induce some oblivion of the highest cause, but when a man passeth on farther and seeth the dependence of causes on the ends of Providence; then according to the allegory of the poets he will easily believe that the highest link of nature's chain must needs be tied to the foot of Jupiter's chair."

It is not until the ruling affection which inspires, and which we term the final motive known only to the Searcher of all hearts, is reached, that the real or ultimate purpose of any act is attained: What we do bears much the same relation to our final motive in doing it that the husk bears to the corn; that the church bears to the worship within it; that the altar bears to the sacrifice upon the altar; that the printed page bears to the ideas expressed by the words on it; that the alphabet bears to the Decalogue; that the body bears to the soul that inhabits it. Every motive, in the last analysis, is an exercise of the will either in harmony or in conflict with the most universally accepted principle of duty, which principle is sometimes and very appropriately designated as Divine. "The fining pot is for silver and the furnace for gold, but the Lord trieth the hearts." [1] Naaman was allowed to bow down in the house of Rimmon because his heart was right and his motive was good. The slave need not fear, "knowing that whatever good thing any man doeth, the same shall he receive of the world whether he be bond or free." So every bondman in his own hand bears the power to cancel his own captivity.[2] The vital question was not whether the disciples ate the shewbread or plucked the corn on the Sabbath, but why they did it. The widow's mite counted

---

[1] *Proverbs xvii. 3.*   [2] "Julius Caesar," Act I, Sc. 3.

for more in the Lord's treasury than all the contributions which the wealthy made from their abundance, not because she was a widow, but because she gave all she had. And she alone of them all, in thus doing, starved every selfish inclination and dedicated every pure affection of her heart to her Master.

The man who had but one talent was not condemned because during his master's absence he had not gained as much as the man who received ten, but because he had not used nor tried to make productive the one he had.

"If the readiness be there," says Paul the Apostle, "it is accepted according to that a man hath, and not according to that he hath not." [1]

---

[1] *II. Corinthians viii.* 10.

CHAPTER V

THE real motive, or final purpose of an act, is not only all of it that is important, but is all of an act that we can with any propriety call our own. We have in ourselves no power to execute, though for wise purposes we cannot divest ourselves of the impression that we have such power. We are in point of fact as incapable of lifting a finger or of opening or closing our eyes as of creating a universe. The very breath of life is supplied to us without interruption, from the beginning to the end of our days, from the Source of all life. The power that sustains us at every successive moment is equivalent to a new creation. To do anything involving our control over the material world, or over any part of it for a single instant, would imply the possibility of more than one omnipotence, which is an absurdity. "Every man is brutish by his knowledge; every founder is confounded by the graven image, for his molten image is falsehood and there is no breath in them." [1]

---

[1] *Jeremiah, li. 17.*

"What man is he that boasts of fleshly might
And vaine assurance of mortality,
Which all so soon as it doth come to sight
Against spiritual foes, yields by and by,
Or from the field most cowardly doth fly!
Nor let the man ascribe it to his skill
That through grace he hath gained victory:
If any strength we have, it is to ill;
But all the good is God's, both power and
    eke will." [1]

"O Lord, I know," said the prophet Jeremiah, "that the way of man is not in himself: it is not in man that walketh, to direct his steps." [2]

"Now it was in the heart of David my father," says Solomon, "to build an house for the name of the Lord the God of Israel: but the Lord said to David my father: Forasmuch it was in thine heart to build a house for my name, thou didst well in that it was in thine heart: notwithstanding thou shalt not build the house; but thy son which shall come forth out of thy loins, he shall build the house for my name." [3]

The lesson here taught has been admirably condensed in a line of the most eminent of the French poets: [4]

---

[1] "Faery Queen," Canto, x, 1.
[2] *Jeremiah, x. 23.*
[3] *Chronicles, vi. 8, 9.*
[4] Corneille's "Horace," Act II, Scene 8. "Do your duty and leave the gods to do theirs."

Faites votre devoir et laissez faire aux Dieux.

The faculty which constitutes our individual life, and the only one which has any pretension to be regarded as absolutely our own, is that by which we are enabled to choose between what we regard as good and what we regard as evil. However powerless we may be to produce or supply the force necessary for the execution of any purpose, we are never without this faculty of electing the motive for doing it, and every motive is resolvable into a choice of what we consider good or evil, or what we consider right or wrong.

The pretexts, reasons, or excuses we assign for our acts which do not involve that alternative are casual, not final. We send our children to school; if asked why, the reason we should be apt to assign would be, "In order to educate them." But why educate them? To give them the better chance in the struggle of life? But why this expense and trouble to qualify others to struggle? Following up the inquiry, we finally reach the point where the real motive is developed. We may do it to promote the happiness and welfare of the child; we may do it to gratify our vanity or ambition, to have the child out of the way, or merely to escape the criticism of our neighbors. Whichever of these or other motives prevail, if we prosecute our inquiry far enough we are sure to come to a good or evil motive which was the real parent of our action. What we do is buried with our bones, but not our motives: they are our real selves; they rise and live on forever. "I know and am persuaded in the Lord Jesus," said Paul, "that nothing is unclean of itself; save that to him who accounteth anything to be unclean, to him it is unclean. The faith which thou hast, have thou to thyself before God. *Happy is he that judgeth not himself in that which he approveth.*" (*Romans xiv.*).

WHAT IS CHARITY?

WHAT IS CHARITY?

CHAPTER I

THE notion of charity which prevails among English speaking people, and, indeed, among most people calling themselves Christians is that set forth by the Apostle Paul in the thirteenth chapter of his First Epistle to the Corinthians, the spirit of which is disclosed in the first three verses of the Authorized Version: "Though I speak with the tongues of men and of angels and have not *charity*, I am become as sounding brass or a tinkling cymbal." The Greek word *agape*, here translated charity, signifies *love* but is rendered indiscriminately in the Authorized Version of 1611 both as "charity" and as "love." In the last verse of the seventeenth chapter of *John*, for example, Jesus is reported as saying: "And I declared unto them thy name, and will declare it: that the *love* wherewith thou hast *loved* me may be in them, and I in them." Here the same word is translated "love" that in the previous citation from Paul is translated "charity." "

In the Revised Version of 1880, however, the

word *agape* is uniformly translated, as it should be, "love." Thus: "*Love* suffereth long and is kind; *love* envieth not; *love* vaunteth not itself; *love* never faileth. But now abideth faith, hope and *love,* these three, and the greatest of these is *love.* Follow after love and desire spiritual gifts." [1]

In Tyndale's first avowed translation of the New Testament, printed in 1534—for which he was imprisoned eighteen months by the English government, then strangled and finally burned at the stake—the word *agape* is translated "love," and as his translation is the basis of the Authorized Version of 1611, the substitution of the word "charity" for "love" by King James' Commission cannot have been made ignorantly or unintentionally. The presumption is that the word "love" in the beginning of the Seventeenth Century in England, expressed a sensual attraction rather than the spiritual attraction which was manifestly in the mind of Paul. It seemed therefore as inappropriate to the context, and in the mouth of the Apostle, as the French word *amour*—the literal translation of which is "love"—would now appear in a French version of the Epistle in question. Happily the word "love" in our literature is gradually resuming the spiritual significance which it had in the mouth of Jesus

---
[1] *I Corinthians, viii.*

and His apostles, and the revisers of 1880, in restoring the correct translation of this crucial word, have made a contribution to the English Bible and to dogmatic theology of no inconsiderable value.

The lexicographers in no instance, I believe, give "charity" as one of the definitions of *agape*. The Greeks had a word which is properly translated "charity," *charis*. It frequently occurs in the New Testament and signifies what is pleasing, charming, graceful, generous, kind, a favor: as when the angel says to Mary (*Luke i.* 28), "Hail, thou that art highly favoured [that is, treated with charity], the Lord is with thee"; and in the thirteenth verse adds, "Fear not, Mary, for thou hast found favour [that is, charity] with God." Paul says in his First Epistle to the Corinthians, chapter xv: "Whomsoever you shall approve by your letters, them will I send to carry your bounty [charity] unto Jerusalem."

In *John i,* 14, 15 and 17 it is written: "And the word was made flesh and dwelt among us, (and we beheld his glory, the glory as of the only begotten of the Father), full of grace and truth. . . . And of his fulness have all we received, and grace for grace. For the law was given by Moses, but grace and truth came by Jesus Christ."

In these verses the words "grace," "bounty"

and "favour" should have been translated "charity" if the word *charis* was in any case to be so translated.   .

It is from the Greek word *charis*, the genitive of which is *charitos*, that we get our word "charity." The Greeks derived it, doubtless, from one of the three graces, whose name was spelled in the same way. The Graces were called Goddesses of Grace and were supposed to confer all grace upon their worshippers and the favor of victory in all games.

CHAPTER II

THE gifts of the wealthy to the poor often, if not generally, produce emotions precisely the opposite of gratitude. The receiver's acknowledgments, if analyzed, would be found to consist mainly of joy at having the gift and contemplation of the pleasure he may expect to derive from it, and very little of gratitude for or admiration of the impulse which the benefactor may be presumed to have obeyed. His motive will be measured by the standards of the receiver. In most cases it gives the latter an acute sense of the difference in his worldly condition from that of his benefactor, and makes of him a socialist or an anarchist.

If his own benevolence is not active, he will be apt to impute the benevolence of others to selfish motives. When Nahash the king of the children of Ammon died, and his son reigned in his stead, King David said, "I will shew kindness unto Hanun the son of Nahash, because his father shewed kindness to me. And David sent messengers to comfort him concerning his father. But the princes of the children of Ammon said to Hanun, Thinkest thou that David doth honour thy father, that he hath sent comforters unto thee? are not his servants come unto thee for to search, and to overthrow, and to spy out the land? Wherefore Hanun took David's servants, and shaved them, and cut off their garments in the midst hard by their buttocks, and sent them away." (*I Chron. xix.* 1-5.) The result of David's kindness to Hanun was a bloody war and the slaughter of some fifty thousand Ammonites.

The trials of poverty, like those incident to the possession of large wealth, are sent to us for a purpose. We are not permitted to thwart that purpose by teaching people to be grateful to us rather than to the Giver of all good gifts who has been pleased to make us His almoner. If their gratitude does not mount to heaven it is apt to turn into envy, jealousy and hate; to breed dissension and distrust rather than brotherly love. As Paul said to the Philippians (chap. iv. 18) : "And you yourselves know, ye Philippians, that in the beginning of the Gospel when I departed from Macedonia, no church had fellowship with me in the matter of giving and receiving but ye only; for even in Thessalonica ye sent once and again unto my need. *Not that I seek for the gift, but I seek for the fruit that increaseth to your account.*" In other words it was the good their sending unto his need had done *them,* not him, that he rejoiced in.

CHAPTER III

PEOPLE most destitute of the comforts of life are the first to murmur at and combine to rob those who exhibit their wealth in charities. They are the first recruits in the predatory army of anarchy and socialism. Instead of being grateful to those who relieve their necessities, they murmur that their benefactors have so much to give.

We are not apt to be grateful for that for which we have not in some way rendered an equivalent.

*   *   *   *   *

When the multitude sitting about Jesus told him that his mother and brethren were without looking for him, He said, "Who is my mother, or my brethren? And he looked round about on them which sat about him, and said, Behold my mother and my brethren! For whosoever shall do the will of God, the same is my brother, and my sister, and mother." (*Mark iii. 32-35.*)

Here a distinction is implied between those who did and those who did not do the will of God. Though His love was over all; though He came, as He said, "not to bring the righteous but sinners to repentance," yet those who did the will of God stood in more tender relations to Him than those who did not. They were His brethren and sister and mother. Others could not come into that relation until they also did the will of God, and for that He was sent. Hence in the model prayer which He gave his disciples He told them always to pray, "Thy will be done on earth *as in* heaven."

* * * * *

We discern with the utmost distinctness a vicious habit in others which we are blind to or wink at in ourselves. Parents deny indulgences to their children of which they partake themselves, though they are equally pernicious to both. We denounce the tricks of partisanship in our rivals or adversaries which we would not only tolerate but encourage in our confederates.

* * * * *

Presents rarely awaken gratitude. The receiver's thoughts turn promptly to the pleasure he will get from them. The wayfarer who slakes his thirst at a spring little thinks of Him who supplies the water. The receivers are gratified but not grateful, as a rule.

This is the trouble with all charity. If people were as grateful for charity as they should be, charity would be merely an exchange. We cannot be grateful for what we have not in some way earned, for we cannot otherwise know its value. In other words, we have to be charitable to appreciate charity in others. We show gratitude to God for our blessings by the use we make of them—want of gratitude by neglecting or abusing them. Man in his best estate ought to have no accumulations of wealth from which to give charity. There is no evidence that Christ ever gave a penny to the poor. He recommended feeding the hungry, clothing the naked, binding up the broken hearted. Every man's environment is best for him, and Christ testified His infinite charity by trying to fit us for a better environment. He did not heal the sick and restore sight to the blind merely that they might live in greater physical comfort, but that they might believe in Him and His mission.

Paul, in his famous instruction about charity (*I Corinthians xiii*) does not once mention the giving of alms or money, but distinctly says: "Though I bestow all my goods to feed the poor and have not charity . . . it profiteth me nothing."

CHAPTER IV

"Whosoever will be great among you, let him be your minister; and whosoever will be chief among you, let him be your servant; even as the son of man came not to be ministered unto, but to minister, and to give his life a ransom for many." (*Matt. xx.* 26-28.) Thus it is that to work for ourselves is to belittle, degrade and impoverish ourselves; to work for others is to magnify, dignify and enrich ourselves. Hence all true, pure, holy, profitable ambition leaves Self quite out of sight and thought. No motive of personal reward or distinction enters into the thought or inflames the heart of the wisely ambitious man. It is what goes out of him, what he does for others that proves his fellowship with Christ; that classifies him with those who would be truly great and who would be chief.

But to work for others, to minister to and serve others, means not to serve merely—nor perhaps at all—their worldly interests, nor necessarily to gratify their desires; it is to do what you think will best serve their highest interest. That may constrain you to thwart their wishes, as is often the case with parents in dealing with their children, of husbands with their wives, and of wives with their husbands. To give money to a spendthrift or to an idler, to countenance a reprobate by concealing your disapproval of his conduct or by any act of charity which tends to palliate or encourage it, is not working at all in the Christian sense for others, and no matter how long or faithfully such efforts are persisted in, they will never satisfy the only ambition which a Christian can afford to indulge. For they are infected with the selfish and worldly spirit which is always looking to some personal advantage, near or remote. Such efforts dry up and shrivel the soul and convert its beauty into ashes.

Christ set up the example of this minstry to others, and His is the only figure in all literature, in history or in fiction, which is not associated with any suspicion of selfishness, which always sought not its own, but another's good. To that model which only the Son of God could reach everyone can approach, and the more thoroughly they are impregnated with the truth taught by our Saviour in these verses to His disciples, and the more they try to incorporate them into their daily life, the greater will be their success and the less unlike to their great Exemplar they will become every day.

* * * * *

When you write a letter to another, or give an invitation, before sending it, ask yourself whether it was for the pleasure or advantage of your correspondent or of yourself, and whether your invitation was intended to promote most your guest's happiness or your own. A careful scrutiny and perfectly ingenuous reply to this question may save you from some disappointment, and also prevent your forming erroneous opinions of your correspondents or guests. If we write and invite for our own purposes, it is well we should know it and be prepared to recognize appropriately and at proper times our indebtedness.

* * * * *

"Another hindrance lies in the resisting earthly stuff in which we must labor, the external and spiritless, the trivial and prosaic which, in a word, is inseparable from all human activity, even the most spiritual, and which becomes even in such a one the most perceptible. Here arises the problem, to breathe spirit into the spiritless. And all human labor, from that of the thinker and artist down to that of the handicraftsman, aims at bottom at impressing by means of the spirit, the stuff that one works; at impressing the stamp of the spirit upon it." (Martensen's "Christian Ethics," p. 302).

That work only is good that is stamped with the spirit—in other words, that contemplates a use by which others will profit. That work alone, too, is easy and agreeable, for the fulfilment of a desire to which our work contributes is always agreeable.

That work is irksome and disagreeable which

does not contemplate some use outside of ourselves, which is not stamped with the spirit—the man turning a wheel while he wishes to be in the ball ground or in a sailboat. But let him reflect that his day's wages will procure for him a new book which he much desires, or a new luxury for his family—better lodgings or clothing for his wife and children—and immediately his heart is in his work; it is stamped with the spirit. The higher and purer the motive, the more cheerfully will he work, for the greater will be its results. The man who works that he may the better minister to the comfort of others, works with more alacrity than he who works merely for his personal enjoyment. For the latter will often steal to secure the pleasure without the work; the former, never or rarely.

If our motives are high, in other words if we stamp our work with the spirit, we will never waste any time or toil, nor will we ever be idle or desire to be idle, and our life in this world will be full of good works and that in the next of their rewards.

This is what is signified by justification by faith and not by works—stamping our works with the spirit. In that is the justification.

"In the truly Christian worker the practical is combined with the contemplative. He works standing in the Christian view of life which is present to him, not only in the quiet hours of contemplation but amid the work itself. And therefore he knows that apart from the result of the work it is not in vain. He knows that, what before and above all else is the Lord's will in our work, does not consist in what we bring to pass, but what we by means of our work ourselves *become*. And then he knows likewise that Divine Providence, without whose will no sparrow falls from the roof, extends also over each true thought, each word uttered in the spirit of truth, each good and well-meant effort, and weaves all this into his great work, although in quite another manner and by entirely different ways from those that lie in our reckoning." (Martensen, Vol. I, p. 303.)

* * * *

"And when they were come into the house, they saw the young child with Mary his mother, and fell down, and worshipped him: and when they had opened their treasures, they presented unto him gifts; gold, and frankincense, and myrrh." (*Matt. ii.* 11.)

What possible good to the infant Jesus, could the gold and frankincense and myrrh be? Of no more good than anything else man can do or give to the Lord. It was good for *them*, however, to make these costly presents in homage to the Day Star which to them had just risen.

CHAPTER V

JESUS was brought to Jerusalem, when the days of His mother's purification were accomplished, to be presented to the Lord, and to offer a sacrifice according to that which is said in the law of the Lord, a pair of turtle doves or two young pigeons. (*Luke ii. 24.*)

This was the sacrifice required of all—no more from the rich than the poor.

* * * * *

When Jesus was told that John had been beheaded to gratify a freak of Herodias' mother, He did not waste a word of regret; He did not propose nor invite revenge, nor organize resistance. "When Jesus heard of it, he departed thence by ship into a desert place apart; and when the people had heard thereof, they followed on foot out of the cities. And Jesus went forth, and saw a great multitude, and was moved with compassion toward them, and he healed their sick." Jesus would not have acted thus if He had esteemed John's murder a calamity to *Him*. He would have set to organizing a revolution to deprive Herod of the power to do such things.

115

Sacrifices and burnt offerings under the Mosaic dispensation were intended exclusively for the benefit of the one making the sacrifice; his purification from evils and falsities. They inured to the advantage of no one else. (*Arcana Coelestia*, nn. 1022, 9959, 10,649, *Apocalypse Explained*, n. 391.)

* * * * *

There is a lesson in regard to charity—especially that of an official character—in the example of Joseph during the famine in Egypt. He made the people pay for the corn in money while they had any, then in stock, and when that was gone, in land. But he gave nothing without an equivalent. Is there any good done to the beneficiary by giving without an equivalent?

The influence of receiving values for which nothing is given in exchange, is one of the most marvelous things to be observed.

The common notions of charity and its supposed advantages to the beneficiary are pointedly rebuked in the twenty-sixth chapter of *Matthew*, verses 7 to 13:

"There came unto him a woman having an alabaster box of very precious ointment, and poured it on his head, as he sat at meat. But when his disciples saw it, they had indignation, saying, To what purpose is this waste? For this ointment might have been sold for much, and given to the poor. When Jesus understood it, he said unto them, Why trouble ye the woman for she hath wrought a good work upon me. For ye have the poor always with you; but me ye have not always. For in that she hath poured this ointment on my body, she did it for my burial. Verily I say unto you, Wheresoever this gospel shall be preached in the whole world, there shall also this, that this woman hath done, be told for a memorial of her."

It will be observed that there is here given a higher purpose and motive for giving than relieving the poor. "She did it for my burial," Jesus says. Wherever the word "burial" is mentioned in the World, the angels understand "resurrection."

To be "buried" signifies to rise again and to continue life because all earthly and impure things are rejected, and not to be buried signifies to continue in things earthly and unclean and for that purpose to be rejected and damned. (*Apocalypse Explained*, n. 659; *Apocalypse Revealed*, n. 506; *Arcana Coelestia*, nn. 4,016, 4,564.)

The widow's ointment was given for His resurrection, for His separation from all earthly and impure things. To contribute towards the resurrection of Christ is to renew a right spirit within us; is to prepare to receive Him and to open to Him the door at which He is knocking.

She gave nothing to relieve any natural wants, such as hunger or thirst, but she poured ointment on His head. Ointment signifies celestial good and spiritual good, or the good of love to the Lord and the good of charity to the neighbor. (*Apocalypse Explained*, n. 375.)

She wrought a good work *upon* Jesus, not *for* him. She contributed to His resurrection in her own heart. Christ did not commend her conduct because of any selfish advantage He derived from it, but because she did something which showed that the dayspring from on high was shining in her heart.

The notion that God is selfish, is to be hired to assist us, is to be propitiated by gifts, seems to infect all the old theologies. One can hardly hear a church service in which it is not assumed that our Father in Heaven "has His price." A chronicler writing of Queen Antoinette from Versailles, May 21, 1778, says:

"Cette princesse a non seulement fait delivrer des prisons de Paris beaucoup de pauvres pères detenus faute de payement des mois de nourrice [the Queen was then in her first *grossesse*] *de leurs enfants, mais elle a dit, 'Si le ciel me fait la grace d'accoucher heureusement, je ferai en sorte qu'il n'y ait plus de ces malheureux.'"* (*Correspondance sur Louis XVI and Marie Antoinette*, V.I., p. 168).

Why did she wait, if the thing was worth doing? She could not have expected ever to have been in a better condition to do it than then. She was not aware, perhaps, that she was animated by purely selfish motives; that she was accusing God of being equally selfish, and what is worse of being under the dominion of motives not a whit more elevated than her own.

It is curious, too, that her proposed trade—for it was nothing else—assumed that putting these people in prison for debt was a great offence in God's eyes, else why assume that He would be propitiated by providing that their offences should no longer be punished in that way? And if wrong, why continue them till after her happy *accouchement* except upon the principle that God was not to be pleased with what was right, but with what gratified His selfishness?

CHAPTER VI

In counseling Henry van Dyke I told him the world loved success and fought shy of the unsuccessful; that he must therefore congratulate himself that he was vice-consul, and need not solicit a professorship as a needy person, but rather as a successful person.

In a certain sense the world is right. The needy person solicits not for the benefit of others, but of himself. He is not going about to do his Master's work, but his own. The world always distrusts the man who is working for himself, just as the man distrusts God; for every man who makes his own gain and not use to mankind and love to God the end and purpose of his actions is wanting faith in Providence, and is trusting to his arm of flesh. Such need to have their confidence in the gods of their own contrivance broken by failure, and the world therefore instinctively, and by a wiser induction than they dream of, is slow to give its confidence to the unsuccessful. By unsuccessful are meant, not the poor, but those who do not succeed in what they undertake. The rich are not always the successful, for they are always wanting more wealth. The poor man who is contented with his lot believes that nothing good in him can suffer injury or decay, and that the Lord is always at his door, knocking and waiting for an invitation to come in and sup with him, and if lifted up from the earth will draw all men unto Him. He is trusted, respected, assisted by all who know him, and beyond his needs.

It therefore generally happens that the man who deplores his condition in life and is constantly soliciting his friends for their influence in his favor, is a man who rarely thinks of promoting the welfare of his neighbor and who never means what he says when he prays, "Thy will be done."

* * * * *

If the incidents of our lives are providentially suited to our spiritual needs, never in wrath but always in love, is there any room for compassion for the unfortunate, or that we should give alms, build almshouses, hospitals, etc.? Rochefoucauld, in his *Portrait Fait par Lui-Même*, says that he was not himself sensible to pity:

"Je suis peu sensible à la pitié, et je voudrais ne l'y être point du tout. Cependant, il n'est rien que je ne fisse pour le soulagement d'une personne affligée, et je crois effectivement que l'on doit tout faire, jusqu'à lui témoigner même beaucoup de compassion de son mal; car les miserables sont si sots, que cela leur fait le plus grand bien du monde: mais je tiens aussi qu'il faut se

*contenter d'en témoigner; et se garder soigneusement
d'en avoir. C'est une passion qui n'est bonne à rien
au dedans d'une âme bien faite, qui ne sert qu'à
affaiblir le coeur, et qu'on doit laisser au peuple, qui,
n'executant jamais rien par raison, a besoin des passions pour le porter à faire les choses."*

POVERTY AND RICHES

POVERTY AND RICHES

CHAPTER I

THERE is probably no more universally accepted notion of what constitutes prosperity and general well-being than the possession of wealth, nor any more universally accepted notion of the absence of prosperity and well-being than that which is expressed by the word poverty. The French call poverty *misère,* a condition to escape which probably more human energy is employed than for any other single purpose.

The best energy of all the so-called Christian nations seems to be mainly occupied, not merely in escaping indigence, not merely in providing for their rational wants, but in assuring such a provision for their posterity, and finally in gratifying an appetite for the accumulation of wealth which grows by what it feeds on. "Enough" pretty generally seems to mean a little more. This "sacred thirst for gold" gives the keynote to most modern legislation and politics and social ambition.

To these appetites may be attributed largely the discoveries and inventions which, during

the last half century, are reputed to exceed in
importance all such discoveries and inventions
made in the preceding two thousand years.
They have been mainly directed to the increase
of man's power of producing wealth or its
equivalent. It is depressing to observe how
much more mental energy is expended in developing the wealth-yielding resources of our
planet than in developing the moral resources
of its inhabitants. This statement finds a
melancholy confirmation in the evolution of
our literature. During the current century, in
most of the natural sciences such as chemistry,
geology, mining, mechanical construction, electricity, agencies for transportation of freight
and intelligence, the progress has been so rapid
that the books in which this progress is re-
corded are superseded by new discoveries while
they are yet damp from the press. The average dime novel has scarcely a less ephemeral
existence than an up-to-date treatise on chemistry or electricity. In contrast with this almost tumultuous activity in the natural sciences,
how comparatively inconsiderable the progress
in any department of moral and spiritual science. The churches seem to have been losing
rather than gaining authority; and fail as a
rule to prove attractive to the first order of
talent, as professions. Books enough are
written, but those dealing with moral energies
and spiritual forces are read by a comparatively limited class.

This extraordinary increase in man's wealth-producing power, instead of increasing the general content and well-being of society, which would be the result one would naturally expect, has been attended by a corresponding discontent among those who have not received what they regard as their share of this increase; and this discontent has not infrequently developed into flagrant and even criminal violation of social order. And strange as it may seem, this discontent has been most conspicuous in countries where the accumulations of wealth have been most rapid and extraordinary.

This war between the Haves and the Have-Nots, though of prehistoric origin, has probably never prevailed so extensively as today; and, it is painful to add, nowhere so fiercely as among the so-called Christian nations. Like war it inflames malevolent, brutal and destructive passions, and like most wars has its origin usually in a common misunderstanding.

There is more than enough wealth in the world amply to supply the material needs of every one of its inhabitants, and there always has been. Let us suppose the world's parliament were to divide that wealth equally among us. That would be the logical compliance with the aspirations of the Have-Nots. There would then be no one to envy; no one to whom, by virtue of his wealth anyone else could look down or up; no one's luxuries to covet, no one's smiles to court, no one's patronage to solicit or resent. Would this be a desirable condition of society? Can we imagine one more deplorable or less in accord with the Divine economy? How numerous the class in every community who would not dream of any other use of wealth but vicious and debasing self-indulgence! Another large class would surrender themselves to a life of thoughtless idleness; a still larger class would toil to possess themselves of the possessions of their idle, dissolute and imbecile neighbors.

To suppose such a state of human society desirable is to assume that the differences in the material condition of its members were ordained, not for any good purpose, but for an evil purpose. To make the social conditions of all equal, it is not enough to give to everyone the same amount of wealth; each must also be endowed, not only with the same intelligence in taking care of and using it, but with the same health, the same strength, the same personal attractions, the same moral character and the same motives of action. Otherwise the more intelligent, the stronger, the more avaricious would possess themselves very soon of the wealth of the less intelligent, the less frugal, the self-indulgent, the idle and the weak, and in a few days or a few weeks the wealth of the world would be distributed as widely, and certainly much more unjustly, than ever before.

It is through the diversities of our condition

in this life that we are educated and that a capacity is developed in us for the enjoyment of another and a higher life into which we hope in due time to be born. How would we ever learn to love one another, to do as we would that others should do unto us, to bear and forbear, to be of any use, if no one had need of anything that we could provide and we had nothing to bestow which any other person lacked? If we ourselves never needed the aid or sympathy of others, nor experienced the emotions which their ministrations to us, or ours to them, might enkindle, life would lack every charm and death would be a welcome change.

It was not without a sufficient purpose that no two persons ever came alike from the hands of their Creator, or ever lived to become a duplicate one of the other, or ever continued for two consecutive days or hours exactly the same person. All life implies change, and none of the purposes of our creation could be realized without it.

The impression that poverty is necessarily of any less importance than wealth in developing man's higher nature, or any less an evidence of God's inexhaustible love for all His creatures, is one of the most regrettable of popular delusions. Everything in Nature is designed by a merciful Providence to teach us laws, the observance of which will secure to us the greatest amount of happiness, not today nor tomorrow perhaps, but in due time. The farmer does not enjoy the cheer of the harvest when he prepares the ground with his plough, nor when he plants the seed. He knows, however, by experience that if he obeys the laws which the Master has prescribed, his seed and toil will provide him with his daily bread in due season.

Our environment, however, has to be readjusted from day to day and from hour to hour, in order that it may be adapted to every variation of our spiritual condition, on which our environment is always operating. Some can resist the temptations which accompany wealth better than others; some can resist the temptations which are incident to poverty better than others. Some need the stimulus of wealth, and some the incentives of poverty. Many lead exemplary and moral lives in the enjoyment of abundance and even luxury, whom poverty would drive to debasing self-indulgence and even to crime; while others, who may be living upon a higher plane, will develop spiritually more rapidly under what seems to be adversity than under seeming prosperity. Both conditions afford opportunities for spiritual growth suited to diverse spiritual conditions, but only the Master knows what we require.

If our bread cost us no toil or forethought we should think no more of the hand that pro-

vided it than children think of the heat and
light of the sun, of the air they breathe, of the
stars in the heavens; we should learn nothing
and we should know nothing because we should
have no incentive to learn anything. All life
would incontinently cease, for life has no more
inseparable attribute than perpetual change.
Indeed, it is one of the great perils of wealth
that it is likely to make us too content with the
present and with things as they are. We are
apt to reason like the rich man who was
favored with an unusually abundant harvest
and knew not where to bestow it. He reasoned
with himself and finally said: "This will I do,
I will pull down my barns, and build greater;
and there will I bestow all my fruits and my
goods. And I will say to my soul, Soul, thou
has much goods laid up for many years; take
thine ease, eat, drink, and be merry. But God
said unto him, Thou fool! this night thy soul
shall be required of thee." [1]

Herodotus tells us the following story of
Polycrates, King of Samos, who was possessed
of a famous ring with magical powers. Amasis,
King of Egypt, persuaded him to sacrifice this
ring because Polycrates, as he thought, valued
it too highly.

"It is pleasant," he said, "to hear of a
friend's prosperity, yet your uninterrupted good
fortune pleases me not, knowing as I do that

_____

[1] *St. Luke xvii.* 18-20.

the Deity is a jealous being, and I could wish
that both myself and those I love should be
fortunate in some of their doings and in others
miscarry, and so pass their lives in changes of
fortune rather than be always fortunate; for I
never yet heard of anyone who with good fortune in everything did not come to a miserable
end. Do you therefore follow my advice, and
do as I tell you. Look out well for the most
precious thing you have and that which you
would most take to heart the loss of, and then
away with it. If afterwards your success
should not take turns and go evenly with your
mishaps, still remedy the matter in the way
here proposed." [1]

In pursuance of this advice Polycrates threw
his magic ring into the sea. Not many days
after, it was brought back to him in the belly
of a fish. When Amasis heard of this, he is
reported to have at once renounced the friend-
ship of a man so clearly marked out for mis-
fortune.

There is no ground for even a presumption
that anyone's happiness is more assured because
of worldly possessions or of the lack of them.

The joys of life are not for the rich alone,
Nor need he grieve who lives and dies unknown.

Our temptations must and therefore always

---

[1] Herodotus III, 40.

will be equal to our powers of resisting them. Wealth brings temptations in one form, poverty in another. Some are constituted with more power to resist the temptations of luxury and power which wealth brings, and some can contend more successfully with poverty. Neither has any substantial advantage over the other. Their chances of spiritual enlightenment are equal. There is no virtue the voice of which may not be heard as quickly by one as the other, whatever may be the difference in the language used to express it. Wealth commands many privileges, but after all does it alone command more than those which poverty develops? Wealth commands university education, books, fine arts, the gratification of our tastes in many ways or degrees and leisure to enjoy them, in some if not all of which the poor share only to a comparatively limited extent. On the other hand, the necessity of earning his bread and the desire some day to enjoy some of the luxuries which seem to him to be the appanage of wealth, incite the poor man to make himself useful to others who can compensate him, that is, industrious, frugal, honest, anxious to win and deserve the confidence of those who employ him and the respect of his neighbors. In time he learns an art or a profession in which he becomes more or less expert, and by means of which he soon makes the wealthy quite as much dependent upon him for what he can do for them that they cannot do, as he is upon them for anything they can do that he cannot. In other words, his poverty is a constant incitement to be useful, and use is the end and purpose of creation. It is Divine worship; it is the happiness of heaven.

"Never be idle," says Jeremy Taylor, "but fill up all the spaces of thy time with a severe and useful employment, for lust easily creeps in at these emptinesses where the soul is unemployed and the body is at ease; for no easy, healthful idle person was ever chaste, if he could be tempted; but of all employments, bodily labor is the most useful and of the greatest benefit for driving away the devil."

That wealth is in itself any more evidence of Divine favor or Divine love than poverty is a fearful delusion.

The Chinese have a proverb that fire hardens mud and softens gold; so poverty may develop one man's spiritual energies and put in ashes another's which wealth might have fostered. When Pharaoh had consented to let the Children of Israel go with Moses, we are told that God led them, not through the territory of the Philistines, though that was the shorter, "lest peradventure they repent when they see war and they return to Egypt and to bondage; but God led the people about, through the way of the wilderness of the Red Sea." The Lord knew what later they discovered themselves, that they needed more the privations of the wilderness for the changes of heart He desired to work in them, than the flesh-pots of Egypt to which they were often anxious to return.

In spite, however, of all that enthusiasts have professed, sages have taught and poets have sung, the mass of mankind have always shown less disposition to get rid of their wealth than of poverty, and have proved capable of more self-denial to acquire wealth than in parting with it. In spite of its manifold graces, the world in general continues to think on the whole more favorably of those who have than of those who have not; generally prefers their society; is apt to extend to them a larger share of confidence. Why is human nature apparently so perverse, so blind to its true interest, so prone, like the foolish moth, to expose itself to the warmth of temptation and the flames of destruction?

The answer to this question is not far to seek, yet it is very important to know.

In the first place, wealth is one of the numerous forms of power of which, through a merciful Providence, man is liable to become a trustee. And the more power we are invested with, the less unlike Him in whose image we were created are we likely to become. Wealth, be it observed, is not the only power of which we may become the trustees that enjoys this distinction, nor by any means the principal one, but it seems unhappily to be regarded as the chief by the greater part of mankind. A power it certainly is when exerted for the purposes for which it is conferred, and for good and sufficient reasons.

As a general thing, the qualities which are most uniformly instrumental in procuring a reasonable measure of wealth, such as integrity, industry, prudence, self-denial, reflection, temperance, patience and brotherly kindness, are precisely the qualities which inspire the respect and esteem of a man's fellow creatures, and which make him a good citizen and a good neighbor, while the reverse of those qualities, untruthfulness, idleness, imprudence, self-indulgence, ignorance, intemperance, impatience and selfishness, all, as a general rule, inspire distrust, discourage friendships, extinguish sympathy and naturally tend to isolate their victims or drive them into association exclusively with companions on their own degraded moral plane. The end of such a career is inevitably poverty or disgrace, one or both, resulting providentially in a corresponding diminution of power and influence.

CHAPTER II

THE people of this world pretty unanimously regard the necessity of earning their bread by the sweat of their brow as a curse. So it was when originally denounced, and so it is now to those, if there are any, who do not need its discipline; but to most of us that necessity deserves to be regarded at least as one of our greatest earthly blessings. That necessity and that only teaches us how to be useful one to another, and compels us to be useful before it would ever occur to us to recognize, still less to obey any such principle of action. Our work under such circumstances has to be useful to others, otherwise it would find no market; in doing such work our hearts and minds are more or less concentrated upon it, and upon efforts to improve the processes and hasten the execution of it. Our thoughts and affections are at the same time—in proportion to the fidelity with which we labor—withdrawn from the more or less morally debilitating meditations and dissipations which idleness always engenders. The luxuries and indulgences which wealth commands are merely incentives to the natural man so to live and labor that he may command them. As they are exhibited to him they seem to represent all that he lacks to be perfectly happy, though wealth of itself confers no more real happiness in this world than the lack of it. The happy man is he who has fewest unsatisfied wants, and the multi-millionaire has in that respect no advantage over 'the humblest breadwinner.

To get our bread by laboring for others is by many regarded as one of the lowest forms of altruism, but whether it deserves to be so regarded depends not upon the work at all, but upon the spirit with which it is done. That is the form adopted by the Master to teach us by degrees a higher form. Hence in this life the young are the learners and the employed; the elders are the employers, not because the elders are more deserving, by any means, but because they have reached a stage of experience when they require a different class of trials or tests for their spiritual development. The average wage earner is without capital either in money, education or experience. When by industry and frugality he becomes more competent, he gets more wages. In time he begins to accumulate capital; with that will come leisure and some of the joys of a broader and a higher life. When he shall have learned to work for others as well as himself, for which such industry was intended to prepare him, and to act from higher than purely selfish motives—with which he probably began—"not looking," as St. Paul expresses it, "on his own things, but every man also on the things of others," he should have no farther need of such a school nor occasion longer to work for wages. He will have converted himself from one of the employed into an employer. His responsibilities will be proportionately increased, his sphere of activities enlarged, and his temptations and tribulations as well as his privileges proportionally refined and subtilized, in order that the process of spiritual growth may continue until Death comes to notify him that this world has no further lesson by which he is qualified to profit.

Those who murmur at the hardness of their lot and the apparent inequality of the ways of God to men, would do well to read the reply which Peter and the other apostles made to the high priest who reproached them for disregarding the orders of the council not to teach in the name of Jesus. "We must obey God rather than men," said Peter. "The God of our fathers raised up Jesus whom ye slew and hanged on a tree. Him hath God exalted with his right hand to be a Prince and a Saviour, for to give repentance to Israel, and forgiveness of sins. And we are His witnesses of these things; and *so is also the Holy Ghost, whom God hath given to them that obey him.*"

We believe in Jesus and in the teachings of His Word just in the degree that we obey His precepts. A light enters the soul and increases in brilliancy just so soon and so fast as we expel from it our self-love, and acknowledge that wisdom and power lie outside of ourselves. The difficulty we encounter in accepting the great truths of the Word and in pressing them home upon others must be due to some common propensity or love which cannot be reconciled with the love of God; and hence our unwillingness to obey Him, without which obedience, as we learn from the language of Peter, the Holy Ghost *will not witness of these things.*

We may have the testimony of Peter and John, of the clergy and Church, but we cannot have the testimony of the Holy Spirit, without which no one's faith is complete and saving, unless we obey Him who sends this witness into our souls. This seems a little like the father's injunction to his son not to go into the water until he could swim. Why should we be expected to obey before we have the conclusive evidence of the Holy Ghost that we ought to obey? The answer to this is not far to seek.

The world in which we are living is governed by inflexible laws, not one of which can be violated without pain, while the faithful observance of them all would be attended with no pain. The pain is a friendly warning that we have missed our way and should retrieve our steps or change our course. If we heed that warning, the Holy Ghost or Spirit will promptly show us the course we should take. If we do not heed it, we shall not be in a frame of heart or mind to listen to the still small voice of the Spirit.

We never perpetrate a sinful act without being notified of the fact by some logical penalty attached to it. If we refuse to pay attention to such suggestions from without us, we should be entirely deaf to the testimony of the Spirit. No one probably ever contracted a vicious habit or lust that he did not often bitterly deplore it; that he did not wish he had listened to the counsels of Peter and John. But their testimony was not sufficient to produce such strength of conviction as insured obedience to the laws of which it warned us. The Holy Spirit therefore could not witness to them of the Christ whom God hath given to them, and to them only, that obey Him.

The story of the Prodigal Son related in *Luke xv. 11, et seq.* is one of the most compendious and impressive illustrations of the uses of poverty in all literature. It tells of a young man craving, as most if not all young men do, sooner or later, to be free from parental restraints, to be allowed to have his own way, and to live exclusively for his own pleasure.

He took the portion of his father's estate

141

which he was deemed to be entitled to, and with it took his journey into a far country—in other words, adopted habits of life widely different from those to which he had been trained under his father's roof. Because the sun was shining bright in that morning of his life, it never occurred to him that it would soon set, and wrap his little, selfish, narrow world in darkness.

Instead of employing his patrimony in a way to make it useful and productive, he wasted it in riotous living and beastly self-indulgence. His Father in Heaven was too merciful and loved him too much to let him prosecute this life of self-degradation farther or longer than was for his good. At a propitious stage in his downward career the lad found himself penniless, homeless, friendless and starving. He was glad to take service as a swineherd and to share the diet of the animals he tended.

It was then, but not till then, according to the inspired narrative, that he realized the error he had committed in leaving his father's house; the infatuation which had led him to disregard his father's precepts and example; the folly, the madness of the kind of life in which he had squandered his patrimony and degraded himself to the level of the brutes with whom he lived. It was then and not till then that, having come to himself, he said: "How many hired servants of my father have bread enough and to spare, and I perish with hunger! I will arise and go to my father, and will say unto him, Father, I have sinned against heaven, and before thee, and am no more worthy to be called thy son: make me as one of thy hired servants." He did as he said he would, for he had told the truth. While leading this dissolute and profligate life he was not worthy to be called or treated as a son of his father.

But when he came to his father, as he did after his avowal of his folly and penitence, and was prepared to give such evidence of his humility as to ask to be received only as a hired servant, his father went forth to meet him, fell on his neck, kissed him, ordered the best robe to be brought forth, put it on him, ordered a fatted calf to be killed, and said, "Let us eat, and be merry."

Now what was the change which had been wrought in this young man which made his father give him such a welcome, make so much more of a demonstration over this penitent profligate than he had ever made over the profligate's brother who had never transgressed one of his commandments?

The reason was that the profligate son had learned by experience how incapable he was of securing happiness by following the devices of his own heart, and how dependent he was upon the advice and example of his father. His selfhood had become so entirely extinct that he had no longer any higher pretension than to be one of his father's servants. He had been so humiliated and emptied of all conceit of himself as to have no will of his own, but simply to serve his father and do his will. But "the rewards of humility and of the fear of the Lord" said the wisest of kings, "are riches and honor and life." This young man now only required to know his father's wishes to do them; to hear his commands to obey them. He now loved his father as he had never loved him before. And by his experience he had also learned the lesson of charity towards others who, like himself, stood most in need of it.

In this respect he had the advantage, we may presume, of the jealous brother who, though he thought he had kept all of the father's commandments, lacked charity for the erring. The penitent brother was now, in the largest sense of the word, regenerated. He had been dead, but was alive again. He had experienced a change for which no amount of wealth or worldly honors would be an equivalent. Yet this new birth into the life eternal was accomplished by a process which the natural man would consider the most cruel and insupportable, by stripping him of all his property, his character, his friends; by degrading him almost to the level of the beasts that perish. His poverty and his deconsideration among his fellows were his salvation.

The getting of wealth is nowhere condemned in the Bible, while the evidences of Divine favor exhibited towards many who were distinguished for their wealth abound. Jeremiah by implication teaches that the getting of riches is all well enough when gotten by right: "As the partridge sitteth on eggs, and hatcheth them not; so he that getteth riches, and not by right, shall leave them in the midst of his days, and at his end shall be a fool." (*Jer. xvii.* 11.)

Abraham was owner of all the land between the Nile and the Euphrates; he also was "very rich in cattle, in silver and in gold." Lot, his nephew, "had flocks and herds and tents;" so many, indeed, that he and Abraham "could not dwell together."

Abraham's son Isaac had possession of flocks and a great household so that the Philistines envied him. His son Jacob had much cattle and maid servants and men servants and camels and asses.

His son Joseph was set over all the lands of Egypt. "Only in the throne," said Pharaoh, "will I be greater than thou." (*Gen. xli.* 40.)

Solomon not only inherited a crown, but was endowed with riches and honor so that there was not any among the kings like unto him all his days. (*I. Kings. iii.* 13.)

When the Lord called Job his "servant," whom the devil could neither tempt nor terrify, he was the richest of all men of the East. (*Job i. 3.*)

Hezekiah had exceeding much riches and honor; and he provided him treasuries for silver, and for gold, and for precious stones, and for spices, and for shields, and for all manner of goodly vessels; storehouses also for the increase of corn, and wine, and oil; and stalls for all manner of beasts, and flocks in folds. Moreover he provided him cities, and possessions of flocks and herds in abundance; for God had given him very much substance. (*II. Chron. xxxii. 27.*) This same Hezekiah "wrought that which was good and right and faithful before the Lord his God. And in every work that he began in the service of the house of God, and in the law, and in the commandments, to seek his God, he did it with all his heart, and prospered."

The Lord was with Jehoshaphat because he walked in the first ways of his father David. He had riches and honor in abundance.

It was a rich young man whom Jesus loved and advised to go and sell what he had and give to the poor. (*Mark x. 21.*)

As Jesus passed through Jericho he spent the night with Zaccheus, who was the chief publican and was rich.

It was Joseph of Arimathaea, who is described by *Matthew* as "a rich man" and as "Jesus' disciple," who persuaded Pilate to give him the body of Jesus which "he wrapped in a clean linen cloth and laid it in his own new tomb which he had hewn out in the rock."

* * * * *

"The stranger and the poor are sent by Jove and slight regards to them are grateful."

There are two things to be noted in this: that even in the Homeric age there were those who realized that poverty was not an accident, nor necessarily a calamity, but was sent by the Supreme Power and therefore for a purpose; and secondly, that the poor are made sensible of their blessings by poverty, for to them slight regards are grateful. It is easy therefore to gratify the poor, but difficult the rich. Therefore the Golden Rule is more easily taught and more readily observed in adversity than in prosperity.

CHAPTER III

When Jesus saw the sick man who had been suffering from an infirmity thirty-eight years, lying by the pool of Bethesda, and knew that he had been now a long time in that case, he said to him, "Wouldst thou be made whole?" The sick man answered him, "Sir, I have no man when the water is troubled, to put me into the pool; but while I am coming, another steppeth down before me." Jesus then said unto him, "Rise, take up thy bed, and walk." And straightway, the man was made whole.

This infirm man had probably blamed the selfishness of his fellow-men for his having been prevented from profiting by the healing waters. He was one of that class who in the competition of life had fallen behind. He had no doubt often comforted himself in the course of his thirty-eight years of suffering with the reflection that he had been very badly used, that the ways of God are not equal; perhaps he had gone so far, as many other unsuccessful men have done, as to question the very existence of a God, or at least of a God with the attributes of love and mercy and justice commonly attributed to Him by His disciples.

At last Jesus saw and spoke to him. Jesus is always trying to speak to us; He is in fact always speaking to us in one way and another, but we are not attending to Him or listening for His voice.

After thirty-eight years of suffering this poor fellow at last opened his eyes, looked up, and for the first time took note of the approach of Jesus, never suspecting probably that no one but himself was to blame that he had not seen Him and been cured before. Then he was cured of his infirmity. Thirty-eight years seemed a long time to him, no doubt, to endure his infirmities, but when he saw Jesus and heard the Savior's words, he realized for the first time that his sufferings were none too long, and that the men who stepped down before him when the pool was troubled were not the responsible causes of his delay in the cure of his infirmity, but rather agents of mercy sent to prolong it until he should discover in his own heart the adversary that was entitled to his reproaches.

*   *   *   *   *

But Abraham said, "Son, remember that thou didst receive thy good things in thy life" (not "in thy lifetime," as rendered in the Authorized Version). Dives received his good things in his life, as being his own, thus natural, not spiritual. His good things are called "thy good things," whereas the "evil things" which

149

Lazarus is said to have received are not called
his evil things but simply "evil things." The
natural man considers all good things as his
own property, and self-derived; not so much the
effect of Divine bounty as of his own prudence,
while the evil things which frequently fall to
the lot of the best men are not properly theirs,
but are only permitted for a time with a view
to their farther purification.

* * * * *

St. Paul, in his first letter to Timothy, makes
an important distinction between those who are
rich and those who desire to be rich. He says
(chapter vi, verse 6):

"But Godliness with contentment is great
gain, for we brought nothing into the world,
neither can we carry anything out; but having
food and covering we shall therewith be content. *But they that desire to be rich* fall into
a temptation and a snare and many foolish and
hurtful lusts, such as drown men in destruction
and perdition. For the love of money is a root
of all kinds of evil; which some reaching after
have been led astray from the faith, and have
pierced themselves with many sorrows."

Later on (verse 17) he adds: "Charge them
that are rich in this present world that they be
not high minded, nor have their hope set on the
uncertainty of riches, but on God, who giveth

us richly all things to enjoy; that they do good, that they be rich in good works; that they be ready to distribute, willing to communicate, laying up in store for themselves a good foundation against the time to come, that they may lay hold on the life which is life indeed."

Here is no complaint of the rich, but of the "desire to be rich." This desire evinces a want of faith, a lack of trust in God; discontent with a condition or environment which is always the best one for us until we fit ourselves for a different one.

There is another lesson in this clause of Paul's letter to Timothy which is apt to be overlooked. It teaches that "the desire to be rich" is no less a folly, a peril and a sin in the poor than it is in the rich.

The "desire to get riches," to which so much evil is attributed, is just as common to the poor as to the rich, perhaps more common. For the rich may have discovered how little wealth has contributed to their happiness—a discovery the poor rarely make. Hence it is probably one of the reasons why so many remain poor.

"He that loveth silver shall not be satisfied with silver, nor he that loveth abundance with increase.

"This also is vanity. When goods increase, they are increased that eat them, and what advantage is there to the owner thereof saving the beholding of them with his eyes?

"The sleep of a laboring man is sweet, whether he eat little or much; but the fulness of the rich will not suffer him to sleep." (*Eccles. v.* 10-12.)

"Two things have I asked of thee; deny me them not before I die:

"Remove far from me vanity and lies; give me neither poverty nor riches. Feed me with the food that is needful for me:

"Lest I be full, and deny thee, and say, Who is the Lord? Or lest I be poor, and steal, and use profanely the name of my God." (*Proverb xxx.* 7-9.)

"He that hath an evil eye hasteth after riches, and knoweth not that want shall come upon him." (*Proverbs xxviii.* 22.)

St. Paul also pressed the folly of regarding riches as an end in life, in his letter to the Philippians who had sent him something for his needs. "I rejoice in the Lord greatly that now at length ye have revived your thought for me; wherein ye did indeed take thought, but ye lacked opportunity. Not that I speak in respect of want; for I have learned, in whatsoever state I am in, therein to be content. I know how to be abased and I know also how to abound; in everything and in all things have I learned the secret, both to be filled and to be hungry, both to abound and to be in want. I can do all things in him that strengtheneth me. Howbeit ye did well in that ye had fellowship with my affliction. *Not that I seek for the gift, but I seek for the fruit that increaseth to your account; but I have all* things and abound," etc. (chap. iv, 10-18.)

"Surely men of low degree are vanity and men
of high degree are a lie.
In the balances they will go up.
They are altogether lighter than vanity.
Trust not in oppression.
And become not vain in robbery;
If riches increase, set not your heart thereon.
God hath spoken,
Twice have I heard this,
That power belongeth unto God.
Also unto thee, O Lord, belongeth mercy;
For thou renderest to every man according to
his works." (*Psalm vi,* 9-11.)

* * * * *

While Gideon was threshing his wheat in the
wine press to hide it from the Midianites, the
Lord appeared to him and said, "Go in this thy
might and save Israel from the hand of Midian;
have not I sent thee?" Gideon replied, "O
Lord, wherewith shall I save Israel? Behold
my family is the poorest in Manasseh and I am
the least in my father's house." The Lord said
unto him, "Surely I will be with thee, and thou
shalt smite the Midianites as one man." And
so he did, as you may read in the sixth chapter
of *Judges,* but before he was sent against the
Midianites he was required to "throw down the
altar of Baal that his father had and to cut
down the Asherah that is by it and build an
altar to the Lord God."

* * * * *

It has been observed that great wealth has
usually been amassed late in life. One reason

153

may be that it then ceases to be of inordinate value to us.

Where great wealth is inherited, it is usually squandered rapidly for a like providential reason, that in this case as in the other it may directly do the least harm and indirectly the most good.

"A good man leaveth an inheritance to his children's children,
And the wealth of the sinner is laid up for the just."
(*Proverbs xiii. 22.*)

*   *   *   *   *

Zaccheus was "a chief publican, and he was rich." He was denounced to Jesus as a sinner by the Church of his day—the Church of which he was also a member—yet Jesus volunteered to be his guest, probably because Zaccheus "sought to see Jesus and could not for the crowd because he was little of stature, and had therefore climbed up in a sycamore tree to see him"; and also, perhaps, because Zaccheus in reply to his denouncers, said to Jesus, "Half of my goods I give to the poor, and if I have wrongfully exacted aught of any man, I restore it fourfold." On hearing this, Jesus said to him: "Today is salvation come to this house. Forasmuch as he also is a son of Abraham." (*Luke xix. 7-10.*)

*   *   *   *   *

In delivering the Commandments of God

154

which the Jews were to observe, Moses adds
(*Deut. viii. 2.*) : "Thou shalt remember all the
way which the Lord thy God hath led thee these
forty years in the wilderness, *that he might
humble thee, to know what was in thine heart,*
whether thou wouldst keep his commandments
or no. And he humbled thee, and suffered thee
to hunger, and fed thee with manna, which thou
knewest not, neither did thy fathers know; that
he might make thee know that man doth not
live by bread only, but by everything that proceedeth out of the mouth of the Lord doth man
live. Thy raiment waxed not old upon thee,
neither did thy foot swell, these forty years.
And thou shalt consider in thine heart that, as
a man chasteneth his son, so the Lord thy God
chasteneth thee."

Moses then set forth the delights that are in
store for those who observe these Commandments in the land towards which they are
traveling: "a land of wheat and barley and
vines, a land of oil and honey, a land wherein
thou shalt eat bread without scarceness, thou
shalt not lack anything in it; a land whose
stones are iron, and out of whose hills thou
mayest dig brass."

Moses then warns them again not to forget
the commandments and judgments and statutes,
"lest when thou hast eaten and art full, and
hast built goodly houses and dwelt therein, and
when thy herds and thy flocks multiply, and

thy silver and thy gold is multiplied, then thy
heart be lifted up and thou forget the Lord thy
God which brought thee forth out of the land
of Egypt, out of the house of bondage, and
thou say in thine heart, My power and the
might of mine hand hath gotten me this wealth.
But thou shalt remember the Lord thy God: for
it is he that giveth thee power to get wealth."

Moses then tells them they are to pass over
Jordan this day, to go in and possess nations
greater and mightier than they, and that the
Lord will overcome these nations for them,
adding, "Speak not thou in thine heart after
that the Lord thy God hath thrust them out
before thee saying, For my righteousness the
Lord hath brought me in to possess this land,
*whereas for the wickedness of these nations
the Lord doth drive them out before thee."*
(*Deut. viii.,* 7-8; *ix.* 2-5.)

Here we have starvation, destitution, and a
prolonged series of trials and tribulations made
the instruments or agents to humble God's
people, to cure them of self-righteousness and
to teach them that they must look up to God
for every substantial blessing, and when these
lessons are learned they will lack nothing ever-
more.

* * * * *

When the disciples, at the command of Jesus,
let down their net after having toiled all night
and caught nothing, they filled their boat until

it began to sink with the draught of fishes that were taken. Peter fell upon his knees and said to Jesus, "Depart from me, for I am a sinful man, O Lord." This confession was the first stage of regeneration. Jesus said: "Fear not, henceforth thou shalt catch men. So when they brought their boats to land, they left all and followed him." (*Luke v. 5-11.*)

These fishermen were poor, probably as destitute of wordly goods as any of the community in which they lived. They would not have fished all night without catching anything if their necessities had not been extreme.

When Jesus came and gave what was wealth to them, their spiritual eyes were opened to see that they were sinners. They were frightened by the discovery. Jesus reassured them by letting them understand that it was just such as they He had come to save. Poverty had done its work with them. Wealth could now do them no harm. They brought their boats to land; *they left all* and followed him. That is, the catching of fish, the accumulation of property had ceased to be an end of life. But to follow Him they left all. Here we see both poverty and abundance employed to lift the hearts of these humble fishermen up from Nature to Nature's God.

CHAPTER IV

Suppose that, though trusting in the Lord and acting according to our best judgment, subsequent events indicate that our judgment was a mistaken one, and we fail. How are we to feel about courses of action that end in failure?

Who made us the judges of success or failure? There is more presumption in judging of the final result of an act than in deciding to perform the act which appears to have led to it, for the Lord has appointed us to judge what we shall do in a present emergency, but He has not given us any capacity for judging which of our acts can contribute most to failure or success in life. Worldly success in many cases proves a spiritual disaster, and the failures we deplore may prove our salvation. If we have not succeeded in life to our expectation, the Divine love may have given us a greater spiritual success than we were capable of asking for, or even of comprehending.

"I will be with thee," the Lord says to each one of us, as He said to Moses when the latter shrank from the mission to which God had called him, and exclaimed, "Who am I that I should go unto Pharaoh and that I should bring forth the Children of Israel out of Egypt?"

"I will be with thee" is addressed by the Lord Himself to each one of us in every stage of life's work. In present perplexities, it means trust and confidence in the Lord. In future threatenings, it means an assurance that nothing can hurt us. In conflict, it means that we shall be victorious. In darkness and despair, it means that the Lord has promised light. In toil and effort, it means that the Heavenly Father will give strength. In pride and self-sufficiency, it means that the Lord will lead us to humility. And in every relation and experience of life it means that we may have the Lord with us, and His infinite love and wisdom sustaining us and enlightening us in all things. "I will be with thee" means that in all life's affairs, great or small, we may have the Divine presence of the infinite Father.

A faithful recognition of the great principle that our environment at any given moment is not only providential but the best possible for us at that moment, should dispel and assuage the discontent, envy and uncharitableness with which the different strata of society are wont to view each other in these days. One is the employer and one the employed; one the master and one the servant; one the merchant and one the clerk; one the capitalist and one the wage-

159

earner; one strong and one weak in body or in mind, not because of man's injustice but because of God's infinite goodness.

No change in our environment could be of any advantage to us unless there were a preceding change in ourselves. We should not repine, therefore, that labor is not adequately rewarded; that our virtues are undervalued; that our station in society is below our deserts; that persons inferior to us in all respects prosper in worldly matters while we have to struggle.

The Israelites were forty years wandering in the Wilderness before they were cured of their idolatrous tendencies sufficiently to be fit to enjoy the milk and honey of the land toward which the Lord was leading them. And yet how much more fortunate were they with all their tribulations than the people they left behind them, with their fleshpots.

Moses, too, shared all their privations and afflictions, not to speak of his graver responsibilities as their leader, which they did not share.

If people would realize that their environment is precisely adapted to their needs; that no one can do anything to their harm but themselves; that they have only to love the Lord their God, the loveliest of all things, with all their heart, and their neighbors as themselves, they would then comprehend the Lord's memorable promise of rest to all who labor or are heavy laden, and His readiness to bear their burdens: how—

"He raiseth up the poor out of the dust,
And lifteth up the needy from the dunghill,
That He may set them with princes."

The Lord would not lift up the poor and the needy and place them among princes if poverty and need were not a soil in which the choicest of Christian graces would flourish. On the other hand, the same inspired authority tells us:

"Blessed is the man that feareth the Lord,
That delighteth greatly in his commandments;
Wealth and riches are in his house, and his righteousness endureth forever.
His heart is established, he shall not be afraid until he see his desire upon his adversary."

* * * * *

We do not desire wealth for its own sake but for what it represents. It can be made to give us power, distinction, finer houses, more luxurious furniture, prominence in the marketplace, but wealth is not the only thing that confers distinction. Public honors of all kinds and degrees have the same origin, offer the same temptations, encourage the same delusions in regard to the true source of these blessings. And instead of prompting us, like the Samaritan leper, to turn back, glorify God, fall upon our faces and thank God for his cleansing, they induce us to behave like the Samaritan's ungrateful companions, who went on their way as though they were indebted to no one for their cleansing but themselves.

* * * * *

The Valley of Achor was the place where Achan was stoned for taking to his own use the spoils of Jericho, which had been devoted to the Lord. Achor is the valley of troubling and Achan the troubler.

The valley of humiliation—a sense of imperfect trust in the Lord, of our inability to contend with the evils that beset us on every hand; the fallacies of sensual and worldly lusts; these may become our door of hope if we only search out what it is that really is the source of our trouble and destroy the accursed thing. That done, we shall experience a new strength, as Israel did after Achan had been found, stoned and his body buried in the Valley of Achor, henceforth to be known as the "door of hope." (*Hosea ii.* 15.)